## PREFACE

First and foremost we are spiritual beings. From time to time we find ourselves in physical human bodies. You are experiencing one of those occasions. But as we shall see, 'life' in flesh and bone on Earth is only a small part of our overall existence. This is just a single small chapter in a far greater adventure.

This book is intended to provide a concise digest of the timeless truths and universal laws which shape us, our world and the universe beyond. As the sub-title suggests, this is merely an overview of a vast and fascinating body of knowledge which offers a coherent and comprehensive explanation of human and cosmic evolution. It does not attempt to explore any of these ideas in exhaustive detail. There are many excellent books available analysing all these subjects in much greater depth and complexity.

Being a general rather than an academic work detailed references have been omitted, although suggested authors are listed at the end. And rather than just focusing on theory – as interesting as this is – this book will attempt to emphasise the practical uses of this wisdom wherever possible. To this end, key ideas and concepts are repeated where relevant.

It is offered at a time when there is an increasing interest in human consciousness and psycho-spiritual development without the prejudices and preconceptions of sceptical science or worn-out religion. It is hoped that it may act as a stimulus to truth-seekers everywhere.

Traditionally, accounts of the Ageless Wisdom begin with the broad expansive theories of cosmic and planetary evolution before looking at human development. But in this book we will reverse that trend and start where we are – at the level of humanity on the physical plane of existence. Because, after all, human beings are small mirror-images of the universe itself. We, the microcosm, reflect the macrocosm in every respect.

You are strongly urged to test every statement made in this book – and indeed elsewhere – against your own knowledge, judgment and most importantly, intuition. At the same time it is always important to be open to new concepts and ideas and where necessary suspend prejudices, pre-existing beliefs or mind-sets.

You may or may not feel an inner gravitational pull towards the Ageless Wisdom.

**Tim Wyatt**, Bingley, November 2016

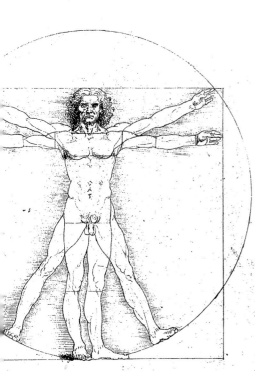

'Man, whose intelligence makes him the one free agent in Nature.'

*The Mahatma Letters*

# 1. IDEAS BEYOND TIME

## ONE LIFE ALL CONNECTED

There is nothing but life in the universe. There are no vast expanses of empty space or inanimate matter. It is a living being and we are an integral part of it. Nothing in it is dead. Although appearing as separate aspects, there is only one life and one consciousness. And we all share it. There is a unity of existence. Everything is part of everything else. We are all one. This is sometimes called *hylozoism*.

We have an immortal soul and we are all part of an eternal journey of evolution – an ageless alchemical process in which over vast periods of time we transmute ourselves to ever higher states of perfection. We have evolved from the lower kingdoms of nature – mineral, vegetable and animal – and ultimately we shall prove ourselves fit for the super-human realms.

We are all 'sparks' of a universal consciousness. The word we use is *monad* which means individual spirit. However, individuality is something of an illusion since we are not apart from anything but an extension of The All or a single supreme consciousness.

The aim of this book is to present a clear, concise and uncomplicated account of knowledge and ideas which have accompanied mankind down the millennia. This is known as the Ageless Wisdom, the Perennial Philosophy, the Universal Knowledge or Theosophy. Theosophy is derived from the Greek words *theo*, divine, and *sophia*, wisdom. It is an ancient blend of philosophy, science and religion – pre-dating them all and involving cosmic laws which shape the evolution of all life in the universe including ourselves.

All nature is sentient. Everything from sub-atomic matter to galaxies is alive, conscious and interconnected and there are states of consciousness and matter beyond the physical plane.

Throughout infinity and eternity there is only one life and a single existence. This means that our home, the Earth is not just a lump of dead rock orbiting the lonely wastes of the solar system in some accidental cosmic dance. It is a dynamic living inter-connected organism with a purpose. We are part of it and it is part of us. The two are intimately interconnected. We deny this truth at our peril.

Crucially, the Ageless Wisdom outlines a panoramic system of ideas and universal laws in which human beings are masters of their own destiny – not some higher power. We rise or fall by our own efforts. We are responsible. All of us are gods in the making.

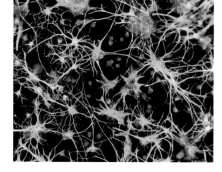

The structure of the universe as seen through the Hubble Space Telescope *(above left)* exactly mirrors that of the brain when magnified many thousands of times *(above)*. This is the clearest demonstration of the fact that the macrocosm is a precise reflection of the microcosm

Most Western spiritual traditions urge us to look beyond ourselves for answers and enlightenment – be they scientific, religious or philosophical. The Ageless Wisdom looks at matters from a different perspective. It focuses on an inward search for a deeper understanding of timeless truths.

For example, humanity is far older than conventional science is yet prepared to admit. Long lost advanced civilizations existed millions of years ago. The Theosophical view is that human beings have been on Earth for almost 19 million years. This is highly controversial from a current scientific point of view. So is much else in the Ageless Wisdom.

There are also worlds, kingdoms of nature and planes of existence hidden from our relatively crude physical senses because they exist outside that physical plane. To gain access to these super-physical worlds we need to develop faculties such as intuition and inner vision to perceive them. Eventually human beings will be born with this wisdom-intuition principle the way they now come into life with sight, touch, hearing, smell and taste. These physical senses only give us the ability to perceive a small part of the overall reality.

Theosophy traditionally uses terminology drawn from Sanskrit and other ancient Eastern traditions. These often convey subtleties of meaning for which there is no direct English equivalent. Wherever possible, this book will use the English words, although terms such as karma (The Law of Cause and Effect) will be retained, since most people have a general (though often misunderstood) idea of its meaning.

This book attempts to provide a simplified summary of this complex wisdom. This inevitably means leaving out much of the minutiae involved. More detail can be found in the primary source books and the many commentaries and interpretations of Theosophy. This wisdom has been remorselessly tested down

## A famous occult maxim

*'As above, so below; as below, so above.'*

This well-known saying illustrates the idea that everything small and familiar to us is simply a reflection of the entire cosmos. The microcosm is an exact mirror image of the macrocosm. An atom is a reflection of a star. Indeed, a human being has been described as 'a universe in miniature'.

'The accumulated Wisdom of the Ages… is the uninterrupted record covering thousands of generations of Seers whose respective experiences were made to test and to verify the traditions passed orally by one early race to another, of the teachings of higher and exalted beings, who watched over the childhood of Humanity.'

HP Blavatsky, *The Secret Doctrine*

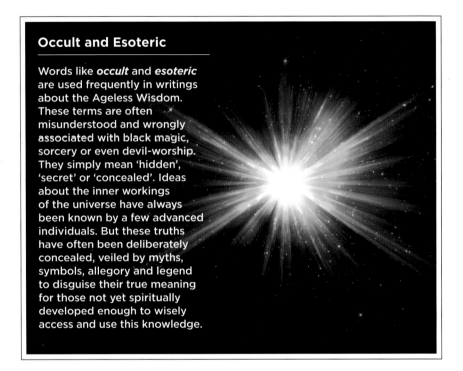

### Occult and Esoteric

Words like *occult* and *esoteric* are used frequently in writings about the Ageless Wisdom. These terms are often misunderstood and wrongly associated with black magic, sorcery or even devil-worship. They simply mean 'hidden', 'secret' or 'concealed'. Ideas about the inner workings of the universe have always been known by a few advanced individuals. But these truths have often been deliberately concealed, veiled by myths, symbols, allegory and legend to disguise their true meaning for those not yet spiritually developed enough to wisely access and use this knowledge.

the millennia by sages, adepts and initiates with a knowledge far in advance of the bulk of humanity.

Unlike religion, Theosophy does not demand worship, blind faith or belief. The Ageless Wisdom puts human beings firmly in control of themselves and with potential mastery over their own development and destiny. It stimulates us to expand our knowledge of the universe, seen and unseen. There are no 'scientific' proofs involved because science confines itself purely to the physical plane and many phenomena occur on other (mainly invisible) levels of reality.

## THE AGELESS WISDOM: A BRIEF HISTORY

For a long portion of human history there has been an advanced knowledge of the secrets of the universe preserved by small numbers of initiates and adepts. Parts of this wisdom are periodically released – often in diluted form. These ideas featured in ancient religions as well as in the various Mystery Schools of Greece, Egypt and the Middle East. They were taught by the Brahmins of India, the Jews in their caves and temples, by Jesus and by Buddha.

In the East, especially India and China, this wisdom has enjoyed unbroken continuity down the ages, lying at the heart of Hinduism and Taoism. Buddhism also offered many elements of this wisdom. In the West, during the first two centuries of the Christian era, many of these ideas were studied by the neo-Platonists and the Gnostics. After their schools were persecuted into silence the wisdom vanished underground for many centuries before reappearing.

In the Middle Ages some of this knowledge resurfaced in the work of magicians and alchemists and later among Kabbalists, Rosicrucians and a number of masonic orders. During the Renaissance, the Enlightenment, the Age of Reason and the Industrial Revolution these ideas again receded, no longer smothered by religion but increasingly marginalised and mocked by influential scientific materialism and so-called rationalism. By the mid-19th Century certain custodians of this wisdom known as the Masters of Wisdom judged the time right to reveal more of this secret knowledge to the world. Among those they selected were Madame Blavatsky, who co-founded the Theosophical Society, as a means of disseminating secrets about the mysteries of the universe – especially to the Western world. Her name appears frequently in this book.

*Below: Composition X* by the Russian painter Wassily Kandinsky (1866-1944), who was a notable Theosophist. Other well-known Theosophical artists include Piet Mondrian, Paul Gaugin, Paul Klee, Nicholas Roerich and Charles Rennie Mackintosh. Many other notable individuals who were influenced by its teachings include Layman Frank Baum, creator of *The Wizard of Oz*, the poet William Butler Yeats, Lewis Carroll, Sir Arthur Conan Doyle, DH Lawrence and TS Elliot. Those in the world of music include Jean Sibelius, Gustav Mahler and Elvis Presley. Mohandas K Gandhi was a member of the Theosophical Society. And the 20th Century's most famous scientific mind, Albert Einstein, is said to have kept a copy of Blavatsky's *The Secret Doctrine* on his desk.

## Helena Petrovna Blavatsky: Godmother of the new age

Helena Petrovna Blavatsky (1831-1891) was a colourful and controversial Russian aristocrat who spent her life travelling to inaccessible parts of the world in a life-long search for wisdom. Her writings form the core of modern Theosophy, especially her chief work *The Secret Doctrine* published three years before her death. This monumental and hugely influential book remains the key source of much Theosophical material, although HPB (as she was and is popularly known) always insisted that she had only 'lifted a corner of the veil'. She not only brought much ancient knowledge to the attention of the West for the first time in centuries, she effectively globalised these ideas, too.

Known as the Godmother of the New Age, Blavatsky was associated with psychic phenomena from an early age. After a brief and disastrous marriage at the age of 17 she travelled extensively to remote parts of Asia including Tibet as well as Africa, Europe, and the United States – remarkable achievements for a woman of the time and especially so for someone who was plagued by illness for much of her eventful life.

During these extensive adventures spanning decades she met various occult instructors including adepts and initiates from a hidden hierarchy of advanced beings known variously as Masters of the Wisdom, mahatmas or members of the Great White Brotherhood. As well as instructing her, these individuals also communicated with her associates and even helped her pen her hugely influential works.

For a woman of refined breeding HPB's behaviour was often abrasive and even unruly. During her life she faced constant criticism and attacks. Like all advanced thinkers she was both revered and reviled. Even today she is still wrongly dubbed a fraud or charlatan. However, many people consider her one of the most profound philosophical minds of the 19th Century.

More than a century and a quarter after her death she remains a pivotal figure and the importance of her achievements cannot be over-estimated. However, we should perhaps regard her as a key pioneer and guide opening up new vistas of knowledge rather than having the final word.

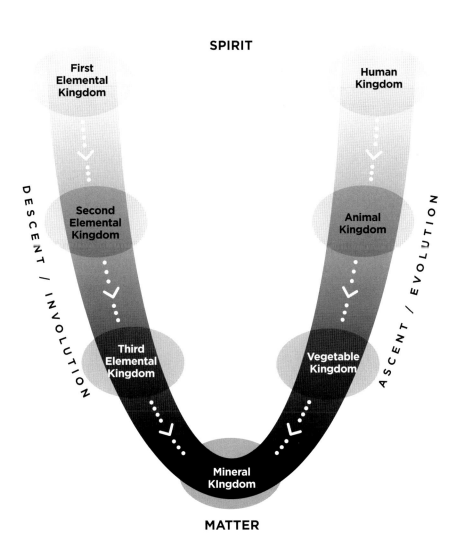

**SPIRIT**

First Elemental Kingdom

Human Kingdom

**DESCENT / INVOLUTION**

Second Elemental Kingdom

Animal Kingdom

**ASCENT / EVOLUTION**

Third Elemental Kingdom

Vegetable Kingdom

Mineral KIngdom

**MATTER**

## Lost wisdom

Wisdom always gets lost and yet it never fully disappears Sometimes it vanishes underground. Often it is concealed in plain sight. Periodically timeless truths are resurrected when they are needed to steer and inspire human progress. In the modern world there is so much data that people speak of an 'information haze' which obscures many important ideas

Wisdom – the absolute unchanging truth about the workings of ourselves and the universe – has always been available to a select few. This wisdom gets gradually diluted into knowledge. Thanks to modern communications systems this knowledge gets further watered down into information, data and then even more degraded into what we might call 'digi-trash'. This is increasingly seen by some as a form of pollution.

### Spirit and matter - involution and evolution

Esoteric writings make frequent use of the words 'spirit' and 'matter'. These are not in any way warring or irreconcilable opposites but different states of the same thing at a particular stage in a long seven-fold cycle. Over vast periods of evolution spirit descends into matter on what is called the involutionary arc. When it has reached its lowest point mid-way through that cycle it begins to ascend on the evolutionary arc as matter is gradually re-spiritualised. So we can regard matter as manifested spirit on the physical plane.

'The World – The Universe is each man's own self, objectified.'

PG Bowen, *The True Occult Path*

## TEN KEY IDEAS

1. **One life.** There is a unity of existence throughout the universe – a single consciousness. Everything, seen and unseen is interconnected and therefore one. This is why it is vital to regard humanity as a brotherhood – at least potentially.

2. **No empty space or dead matter.** Every part of the universe is teeming with life. Everything visible and invisible is a conscious life-form. Even atoms have consciousness.

3. **An infinite universe.** With neither beginning nor end, the universe is eternal and immortal undergoing endless cycles of spiritual as well as physical evolution – although it undergoes periods of activity and corresponding periods of rest. This notion of evolution differs somewhat from the way mainstream science describes it.

4. **Universal Laws.** The cosmos is governed by a series of hard-and-fast laws, the chief one being The Law of Cause and Effect, popularly known as karma. This teaches us that every cause has a resulting effect either now or in the future. Everything we do, say, think or feel has a future impact positively or negatively. We cannot avoid this. Our words and acts shape our future progress.

5. **Reincarnation.** This is the means whereby human beings repeatedly return to human bodies in order to gain experience – based on the activities of previous lives. Reincarnation without the over-arching Law of Cause and Effect would be meaningless.

6. **A seven-fold universe.** There are seven planes of existence, seven key forces in the cosmos and seven states of consciousness. This applies to everything including human beings. But they still remain different aspects of the one life.

7. **Death is a myth.** Nothing dies. But as part of its cyclic activity all things from a sub-atomic particle to a galaxy exist for a time in non-material states.

8. **Cycles.** Everything is cyclic – from a single heartbeat to the entire evolution of a galaxy. Some cycles last a fraction of a second. Others last trillions of years or more. All life proceeds through the same cycle of birth, growth, maturity, decline and death. There are no exceptions to this.

9. **Evolution.** Everything is part of an infinite evolutionary process covering enormous time-scales and includes life in both physical and invisible worlds.

10. **A Grand Plan.** Life has a purpose. It is neither random nor accidental but part of an overall scheme sometimes called The Divine or Grand Plan.

## EIGHT BASIC LAWS

1. **The Law of Periodicity:** After every period of activity there is a rest interval. This is seen in birth and death, waking and sleeping, day and night or the ebb and flow of tides. This also includes The Law of Constant Renewal as demonstrated in the necessity for rebirth and re-embodiment.

2. **The Law of Adjustment:** This is to ensure that whenever harmony is disturbed, adjustment has to be made to restore equilibrium and balance. The action of this is illustrated by The Law of Karma.

3. **The Law of Essential Unity:** Every entity lives its life in the sphere of influence of a greater being. Throughout the universe there are infinite hierarchies of life.

4. **The Law of Self-Unfoldment:** This underscores the urge of every entity to express itself in line with its essential characteristics.

5. **The Law of Motion:** Everything in nature is constantly on the move. Nothing is static. There is always constant change. Entities are always striving for a loftier status.

6. **The Septenary Law:** This is central to esoteric thinking. There are seven planes of existence. Human beings have seven bodies. There are seven root races (or development groups). On a more everyday levels there are seven days to the week, seven colours of the rainbow and seven notes on the musical scale.

7. **The Law of Compassion:** Compassion exists throughout the universe. The cosmos is not the selfish, separated place some scientists imagine and compassion is crucial to the carrying out of The Divine Plan.

8. **The Law of Coming Into Being:** This law illustrates that there is nothing but life in the universe. Life pervades every entity large or small, seen or unseen.

## THREE FUNDAMENTAL PROPOSITIONS

This trio of ideas appears in HP Blavatsky's *The Secret Doctrine*.

a.  An Omnipresent, Eternal, Boundless, and Immutable PRINCIPLE on which all speculation is impossible, since it transcends the power of human conception and could only be dwarfed by any human expression or similitude. It is beyond the range and reach of thought…

b.  The Eternity of the Universe in toto as a boundless plane; periodically the playground of numberless Universes incessantly manifesting and disappearing, called 'the manifesting stars', and the 'sparks of Eternity'… The appearance and disappearance of Worlds is like a regular tidal ebb of flux and reflux.

c.  The fundamental identity of all Souls with the Universal Oversoul, the latter being itself an aspect of the Unknown Root; and the obligatory pilgrimage of every Soul – a spark of the former – through the Cycle of Incarnation (or 'Necessity') in accordance with Cyclic and Karmic law, during the whole term.

*Above:* The frontispiece of HP Blavatsky's *The Secret Doctrine*, first published in 1888 and which has remained in print ever since. Although difficult to read, the book continues to have a major influence on modern esoteric thinking.

'Nature is not a fortuitous concurrence of atoms.'

HP Blavatsky, *The Secret Doctrine*

## ACCIDENT OR GRAND PLAN?

Did the universe come into existence through accident or design? This is at the very heart of an ongoing debate in the modern world.

In the early 21st Century the prevailing view certainly in the West is that the Universe came into existence around 13.8 billion years ago as the result of the (as yet still theoretical) Big Bang. Through a series of random accidents, cosmic collisions and coincidences the universe and all its life-forms underwent various stages of evolution as outlined by the (also unproven and incomplete) theories of Charles Darwin in the 19th Century.

Many scientists see no fundamental purpose to any of this epic development. It just happened for no particular reason. Science can explain the mechanics of how things happened but not why. Scientists are extremely reluctant to speculate on the meaning of life.

Theosophy and other interpretations of the Ageless Wisdom argue that there is both consciousness and purpose to the evolution of the cosmos and ourselves. In other words, there is a Grand Plan or Divine Scheme which is unfolding. We play our part in this plan whether we are aware of it or not. Understanding that we can be active and creative participants in this scheme represents a huge leap forward in our own self-development.

### All in it together

One fundamental idea is that all entities live within the body of a greater being. Atoms are part of molecules. Bacteria live as part of bigger organisms. Everything on Earth is part of a greater planetary spirit and each planetary spirit in our system is part of a solar spirit. Beyond that are even more evolved entities.

'The universe is a thought of God.'

Franz Hartmann, *Magic White and Black*

'God does not play dice.'

Albert Einstein

## WHAT ABOUT GOD?

When people use the word 'God' they mean many different things. This often depends on which religion they belong to or whether they believe in such a concept in the first place. Many people, even those pursuing spiritual paths, often feel very uncomfortable with the word because of its ambiguities or religious overtones.

For most Christians God is a man, a very elevated man, who can show favour or punish, depending on how we behave. They hold to this view because The Bible teaches that God made man in his own image.

The Ageless Wisdom tradition rejects all notions of an anthropomorphic or human-like God, preferring instead to use terms such as The Absolute, Universal Consciousness, Superintelligence or The Divine Mind which is infused in everything.

Theosophy is totally opposed to the idea of a personal, angry and often vengeful God as portrayed by Jehova in the Old Testament or Zeus in the Greek myths. In this view – shared by other religions – human beings are weak, innately sinful and entirely powerless. God knows best and has the right to torment us. Theosophy takes a more liberated stance, believing that human beings themselves hold the keys to their own futures. And since everything is intimately interconnected, the divine or spiritual is infused into everything and we cannot make the separation between the divine and ourselves.

Does this Super Being demand to be slavishly worshipped and adored? Does The Absolute need propitiating with dogma, ritual – and even the sacrifice of living creatures? Perhaps he does not stand on ceremony the way some people imagine. And maybe he does not want to make us suffer. Possibly his only wish is that we co-operate with and participate in The Grand Plan.

The three chief religions of the West (sometimes called the Mosaic religions) Christianity, Judaism and Islam (which in fact share more common ground than issues which divide them) believe there is one God, one earthly life and an infinity spent in the pleasant recesses of Heaven or the fiery ravages of Hell. Eastern religions take a different view. Buddhism and Hinduism believe in an over-arching power but the active evolutionary work is in the hands of lesser deities. Hinduism, for example, has a massive pantheon of some 330 million spirits and demi-gods.

*Left:* A stereotypically human interpretation of 'God' by the English mystic, poet and painter William Blake. Biblical notions that God made man in his own image have created centuries of confusion.

## THE MYSTERY OF CONSCIOUSNESS

In one sense there is nothing but consciousness anywhere in the universe. Everything is conscious on its own level. Consciousness is energy. And energy underpins matter. So matter is conscious.

Unlike the lesser kingdoms of nature human beings have the capacity of self-consciousness. We operate on the mental plane and we create with our minds. It is often said that thoughts are things. Although much finer than physical matter, mental matter does create its own structures, some transitory and some long-lasting. So whenever we think we create thought-forms.

As sophisticated as science has become, it still cannot either explain or define exactly what consciousness is. It still regards consciousness in wholly physical terms. Most scientists still insist that the brain is the sole seat of consciousness. Their view is that mind and brain are interchangeable and that our consciousness is purely a product of the electro-chemical action in our cerebral cortex.

Other cultures believe that consciousness is located in the heart. Theosophy stresses that the mind exists beyond the physical brain on other much more subtle planes. In fact it does not require a brain at all. Science teaches that form produces life and consciousness. Esotericists believe the exact opposite: that consciousness produces material existence. When you explore this idea you see that everything has its origin on the non-physical planes.

The majority of human beings are ruled by their desires for material goods, wealth, fame, status, recognition and emotional gratification. These are the very things we are closely conditioned to believe and not question. And yet desire is the chief obstacle to real spiritual progress because it anchors and attaches us to lower planes of existence and impedes our discovery and exploration of higher realms.

Theosophy divides the mind into two parts: lower and higher. The lower is part of the transient personality while the higher is part of our permanent individuality which continues throughout different incarnations (although modified by them).

'…whatever plane our consciousness may be acting in ... both we and the things belonging to that plane are, for the time being, our only realities.'

HP Blavatsky, *The Secret Doctrine*

*Above:* Consciousness, as represented by alchemist, Robert Fludd, from the 17th Century.

'For occult science, intelligence came first, but for Western science, intelligence comes last – as the culmination of the ladder of evolution and being essentially the product of molecular activity in the human brain.'

Edi Bilimoria, *Mirages in Western Science Resolved by Occult Science*

## SCIENCE AND SPIRIT

This book makes the distinction between mainstream science and its much older ancestor, occult science which was developed over millennia by adepts and esoteric investigators but unknown to the world at large.

For many people science and technology are the new religion. Science has certainly widened our understanding of ourselves, our world and our universe but despite its huge achievements it remains limited by its own thinking. And let us remember that like everything else it is itself evolving. It has no final answers. It remains a work in progress. Nevertheless, as HPB observed, science may be our best hope – but only if it expands its own consciousness beyond the physical dimension. This is gradually beginning to happen.

### Collective consciousness in action

We generate fields of consciousness both knowingly and automatically as well as individually and collectively. These produce auras and atmospheres you can often feel at big gatherings such as concerts, sports events and at religious or political meetings. In riots and wars collective consciousness frequently influences the behaviour of those involved. It inspires some to acts of sacrifice, compassion and heroism. In other situations previously mild-mannered people turn into monsters committing slaughter. It is often very difficult for individuals to operate against the collective mind because it becomes so powerful.

Collective consciousness has a profound effect on events and on ourselves - be they fashion fads, cultural phases or political or religious ideologies. It is clearly seen in crowd behaviour, mass hysteria, rumour, myth and legend.

However, the collective mind is also creative - and most likely predictive. For example, imagine putting 1,888 sweets in a jar and asking a group of people to guess the number. Some would say there are 50 while others would estimate a figure beyond 10,000. Interestingly, if you were to take the overall figure from 50 individuals, add it together and then divide that number by 50 you would receive a remarkably accurate guesstimate. The higher the number of people guessing, the more accurate the aggregated figure. This accuracy is a product - or rather a process - of the collective mind, not that of the individual.

Since the late 20th Century the Institute of Noetic Science (IONS) has carried out fascinating and rigorous research into group consciousness as part of its Global Consciousness Project. It measures this by using random number generators (RNGs) at dozens of locations around the world. It has discovered that important local events affect these devices which then no longer act randomly. In events of major global significance such as the death of Princess Diana in Paris in 1997 or the attacks on the World Trade Centre twin towers in New York, IONS discovered that RNGs around the world all reacted and stopped behaving randomly. Intriguingly, the machines began to respond before these events actually occurred.

Technology has produced a world revolution in travel, healthcare, manufacturing, food production, information technology and many other areas of human endeavour. But its products can become objects of fetish worship be they cars, digital communications devices or even household gadgetry. And it has given us the ability to destroy ourselves in a number of ways.

The danger is that we become enslaved by and dependent on the very technology we hoped would liberate us.

The problem is that modern science is based solely on the notion that only physical matter exists and there are neither super-physical nor spiritual realms. What you see is what you get. The Ageless Wisdom hugely expands these horizons.

This narrow scientific view has led not to a wider understanding of reality but an ignorance – and some might argue, an arrogance.

Over the last 250 years Western science has undergone increasing specialisation into compartmentalised sub-disciplines which very often cannot communicate with each other – let alone the outside world. These disciplines all develop their own language. For example, astrophysicists often cannot speak to biologists, although this is also beginning to change.

Science has a lot to say about the 'whats' of existence but virtually nothing about the 'hows' or 'whys'. This is because it concentrates its investigations solely on the physical plane ignoring six other planes of existence.

Much of what science teaches are still theories not laws – the Big Bang, Darwin's Evolution, Einstein's Theory of Relativity. But it behaves as if these are universal proven principles.

However, the Big Bang is not necessarily incompatible with the Ageless Wisdom tradition which teaches that as part of lengthy cycles (*manvantara* in Sanskrit) worlds emerge and then vanish into a period of suspension and rest (*pralaya*). Perhaps this Big Bang is a regular occurrence cosmologically speaking.

In its bid to unlock the constitution of matter and the origins of the universe science continues to resort to more and more grandiose and expensive physical hardware, which it hopes will reveal the cosmic building blocks. They have proved very popular – especially among scientists since they provide thousands of jobs and the chance to enhance academic reputations.

Whether The Large Hadron Collider, a 27 kilometre circular particle-cruncher running beneath France and Switzerland, will be a multi-billion dollar indulgence or may reveal real answers remains to be seen. Unless and until science forsakes its exclusively physical/material perspective its explanations can only remain partial.

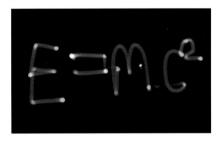

' For the past century science has been moving away from its mechanistic interpretation of the universe towards a more esoteric viewpoint… Quantum theory thus reveals a basic oneness of the universe.'

Fritjof Capra, *The Tao of Physics*

## A meeting of opposites

Science and spirituality are destined to converge. We shall develop a scientific spirituality and a spiritual science. Some of it is happening already with a few mainstream scientists risking their reputations to embrace aspects of the Ageless Wisdom tradition.

Indeed the two different camps may eventually evolve a common language. However, science has reluctantly admitted that it cannot in fact see around 93 per cent of the universe. The hidden portions are described as dark energy and dark matter. These probably correspond with the etheric and astral planes spoken of in Theosophy and the ancient knowledge tradition.

Increasing numbers of experiments are showing the inter-connectedness of our world and our universe and modern genetics clearly demonstrates that all life is intimately inter-related. Studies in consciousness and *noetic* (from the Greek 'nous' or mind) sciences are gradually gaining greater acceptance. But mainstream science has remained obdurate and cynical in its attitude.

Nevertheless, down the centuries many influential scientists and thinkers have studied esoteric ideas and have often been heavily influenced by them. Studies in quantum physics, which began in the early part of the 20th Century, are still causing major reverberations in modern scientific thought and emerging ideas about the constitution of matter are beginning to show parallels with the Ageless Wisdom teachings.

On the plus side, discoveries in quantum physics are revealing a world uncannily similar to that outlined by ancient esoteric thinking. After all notions of 'quantum entanglement' seem very similar to the one-life-in-the-universe concept – not to mention karma, the Law of Cause and Effect.

These inter-penetrating fields of activity where everything is connected to everything else have been called 'morphogenetic fields' (a term coined by the biologist Rupert Sheldrake) or 'zero-point energy'. They seem identical to the way in which the Ageless Wisdom regards these 'matrices of existence'.

The current holy grail of science is to form an over-arching explanation of how the very small and very large knit together into a whole. However, a Grand Unified Theory (GUT) or Theory of Everything (TOE) remain elusive.

## Maya and the illusions of self, time and space

Our view of the world around us is almost exclusively shaped by our limited physical and mental perceptions. We are brought up to believe that 'seeing is believing'. But we know even from contemporary science that what appears as solid matter is in fact quite the opposite. And quantum physics has opened up very weird and unexpected vistas in the microscopic world. Astrophysicists, too, are making huge advances in their analysis and mapping of the universe. It appears very different to the cosmos of a few decades ago.

Human physical senses work only within a very confined part of a wider spectrum. Many birds and animals have far more acute hearing and much better sight than we do. Some non- human species' sense of touch, taste and smell is also far more developed than ours. It often needs to be for their very survival and evolution.

Our mental equipment has improved exponentially in recent centuries thanks to greater communication and interaction, social improvements, better life expectancy and, of course, improved education. It is said that in 16th Century Shakespearean England, peasants on the land had an average vocabulary of around 400 words, the equivalent of a small child today.

Our intellectual abilities have improved but much of this is still mainly focused on the lower mind of mundane and concrete thoughts. Our loftier thoughts and spiritual aspirations often remain straight-jacketed. One of the chief downsides of these limitations is that it reinforces an entirely false sense of self – a separated entity working in isolation from everything and everyone else. This in turn produces greed, acquisitiveness, over-development of the little ego, competition and many other negative traits. This sense of self is an illusion.

Another illusion is time. Time only exists here on the physical plane. Our use of it as a convenience hinders our understanding of it. We regard time as linear and sequential beginning in the past, flowing through the present and existing as a potential in the future. Although we and the universe undergo cyclic evolution, it takes place in what could be called an eternal present. Everything that has ever happened or will ever happen is happening now and will always happen. This is a very difficult idea for most of us to grasp.

*Maya* is a commonly used Sanskrit word often simply translated as 'illusion' but more accurately it means the illusory nature of human thought as we try to interpret the universe. And along with our inaccurate notions of self and time, the way we perceive space is also illusory, too.

## THE MEANING OF LIFE

Ever since human beings first developed mind, the world's thinkers have spent millennia pondering age-old and key questions such as:

- *Who are we?*
- *Why are we here?*
- *Where did we come from?*
- *Where are we going?*
- *What is the purpose of existence?*

The short answer to all these questions is that we are part of an everlasting evolutionary process in which our mission over many hundreds or thousands of lives in physical bodies is to progress and develop in line with cosmic law and an overarching grand plan. We travel through the various kingdoms of nature so that minerals become plants which evolve into animals which ultimately become human. Humanity's aim is to reach the superhuman realms (sometimes called the Fifth Kingdom) of spiritual knowledge and achievement. Each one of us is part of an audition for godhead.

We achieve this through a series of initiations, each one proving a greater mastery over ourselves. An initiation is simply a significant increase in consciousness. And remember that consciousness exists on all planes of existence – not just the mental.

Both science and religion offer different and often violently contradictory views to these questions. For example, science holds that the world came into being and has evolved accidentally with no over-riding guiding plan. Most religions say all existence is the work of God. The Ageless Wisdom offers a coherent synthesis and extension of both these key positions. Crucially, it puts human beings at the very heart of evolution – and not as passive, sinful victims.

So the Ageless Wisdom offers a liberation from these fixed and limited ideas which have shaped human thinking and constricted human psycho-spiritual development. It recognises that each one of us has enormous potential for evolution.

How vigorously we decide to accelerate this growth is entirely up to us – and depends exclusively on our own efforts.

# 2. LIFE ON EARTH

## INTRODUCTION

In this section we will be exploring the way that life operates here on Planet Earth in forms and realms both detectable by and invisible to our physical senses. We will look at the various kingdoms of nature and the way human beings really operate – not only in their physical bodies but in their other subtle vehicles. As we will discover, our physical home is a far more complex place than most people imagine.

As we will see in this and other sections there are planes of existence beyond the physical such as the astral and mental planes. Potentially we can consciously access some of these other realms, although not always the highest.

1 Divine

2 Monadic

3 Spiritual

4 Intuitional
(Buddhic)

5 Mental

6 Astral

7 Physical / Etheric

## SEVEN COSMIC PLANES

The universe itself can be divided into what are known as seven planes of being or more accurately states of consciousness. All these are the result of energy in motion vibrating at different rates. Each plane is made of different densities of substance – with the highest rate of vibration producing the finest substance at the spiritual level and lower rates producing the denser substances of the lowest physical plane. These planes are all sub-divided into seven sub-planes.

We are able to perceive forms and objects on the physical plane through our physical senses but on the higher planes of the astral, lower and higher mental worlds as well as the spiritual these are invisible to our physical sight. (However, some individuals are able to operate in the astral and mental realms. Those able to access the astral plane see images as star-like, watery and constantly changing shape.) The astral plane gets its name from the Latin word for star *astrum*.

The transition points at which the substance of one plane disappears and re-emerges as the lowest sub-plane of the plane above are sometimes known as *laya* centres.

The four highest planes – the Intuitional, Spiritual, Monadic and Divine are known as formless planes. It has to be said that our knowledge of these rarefied areas is flimsy and our knowledge incomplete and our 'bodies' on these planes are not finely organised. The lowest planes – the physical, astral and mental – are composed of substance and form, although the highest mental matter might be considered as fine dust whereas the lowest physical could be represented by large rocks.

Apart from the physical, all the other planes are effectively invisible worlds. And even the densest physical matter has been shown by scientific observation to be far from solid.

## SEVEN STATES OF MATTER

Generally we regard physical matter in terms of solids, liquids, gases and possibly plasma (super-heated gas). However, there are increasingly finer states in this physical spectrum known by Theosophy as the etheric states. These etheric states are not yet recognised by science but it is widely anticipated that they may well hold the key to future energy, healing and other advanced technologies.

There are a number of distinct opinions as to exactly where the etheric states (sometimes known as etheric, sub-etheric, atomic and sub-atomic) reside in this spectrum. One interpretation is that the etheric is part of the physical plane. Another is that it is part of the astral. The important point is that it is the link between the two planes – an organising field for the formation of matter.

Later when we look at the human constitution we shall see that the human body has an etheric counterpart or double. This is the means by which energy and vitality animate the physical body. Each of these sub-planes of physical matter gets increasingly finer from the solid to the atomic. And beyond the physical plane, the astral and mental worlds are made up of yet finer material.

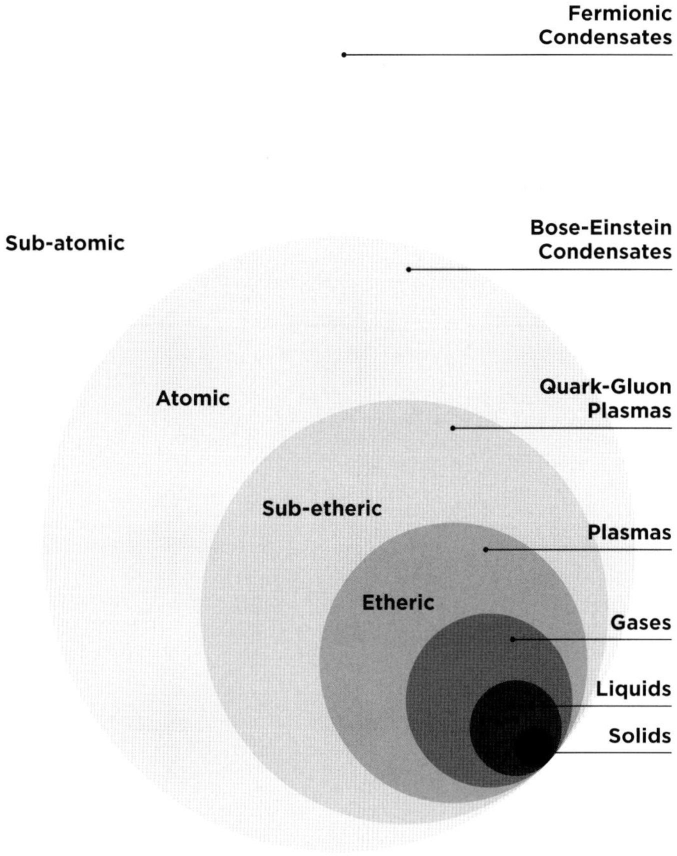

Fermionic Condensates

Sub-atomic

Bose-Einstein Condensates

Atomic

Quark-Gluon Plasmas

Sub-etheric

Plasmas

Etheric

Gases

Liquids

Solids

## SEVEN KINGDOMS OF NATURE

We normally divide life on Earth into three categories: animal, vegetable or mineral. But this is a very incomplete picture.

There are at least seven distinct kingdoms in nature – and more than that if you include those above the human. And each of these kingdoms is sub-divided into many types, genii and species, all at different stages of evolution. For example, the highest point of evolution in the mineral kingdom might be a crystal such as a diamond or sapphire. In the vegetable or plant kingdom, a thousand year old oak tree is more evolved than a lichen or a weed.

It is important to remember that all kingdoms of nature have consciousness – even rocks. Certainly the vegetable kingdom shows active intelligence with many trees and plants displaying sophisticated means of communication (sometimes over

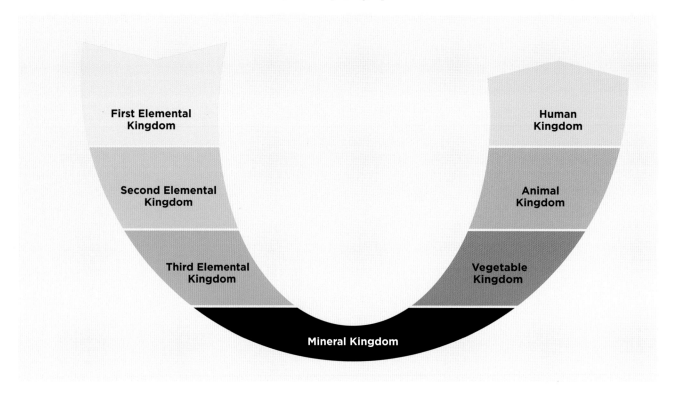

considerable distances) to warn other members of their type that predators such as insects are on the way.

Everything evolves from everything else. After huge periods of time minerals become members of the plant kingdom. Plants ultimately evolve into animals. Animals eventually join humanity. And humanity itself is destined for loftier things. Our ultimate future is in the many hierarchies above the human. It is often said that we are gods in the making – however difficult this is to believe at the present time. (We will deal with this in the section on **Hierarchies**.)

The Ageless Wisdom is very clear that humans are not highly-evolved members of the animal kingdom – super-apes – but part of an entirely different stream of development. We are the only self-conscious kingdom (although some animals do possess a basic form of self-consciousness as many pet-owners know.) And we are the only one with individualised souls.

The human kingdom is the pivotal, energising department of nature – the creative (and destructive) genius which impacts so much on all the other kingdoms. A turning-point is being reached where humans are beginning to understand the intimacy of their relationship with the natural world. We are seeing more initiatives to work with rather than against nature. We are slowly realising that mankind can positively assist the development of other kingdoms rather than merely exploit them.

Significantly, humans do possess remnants from the kingdoms through which they have progressed. Much of our physique and perceptual equipment is direct from the animal kingdom, especially mammals. Our lymphatic system (tissues and organs which rid the body of toxins) bears many resemblances to the plant kingdom. And our bone structure and teeth are minerals.

## Views of evolution

The Theosophical view of evolution is different from both Darwin and the Biblical Creationists, although it shares some aspects of both.

From the Darwinian standpoint evolution happens through natural selection via mechanisms such as 'survival of the fittest' in which the kingdoms of nature adapt to changing environments. And yet exponents of this view insist that it is all a random, if not an accidental process with no plan or purpose behind it.

Creationists with a literal understanding of The Bible believe that God created the world in six days – possibly as recently as 4,004 BCE – all by himself. But they also fail to say why terrestrial evolution was set in place – especially since Christians of this type view man as innately wicked and sinful.

The Ageless Wisdom tradition says that the universe has always existed and always will but that it undergoes regular periods of visible activity and unseen rest. In other words, it comes in and out of physical manifestation. Since the universe consists of the many aspects of the One Consciousness it is created through hierarchies of entities and a variety of agencies through endless cycles and spirals of development. Crucially, Theosophy informs us that despite periodic local difficulties such as war, conflict, natural disasters and cosmic forces, everything is proceeding roughly according to a grand plan.

## Hidden power

In the modern Western world the idea of hierarchies is becoming an increasingly unpopular one. They are seen as wielding too much control and not acting in the best interests of people – especially in the world of politics and big business. But these are transient, false and self-serving hierarchies usually based on power, greed and manipulation.

The true hierarchy of this planet does not seek to coerce or steal from anyone. It has only humanity's evolution at heart. Under universal law – rather than human law – it seeks to use its experience, expertise and advanced state of evolution to carry out the divine plan in spite of transient problems.

## HIERARCHIES

The universe consists of numerous hierarchies of life. The Earth has a far-reaching system of hierarchies and so does the wider solar system, although our knowledge of this is very far from comprehensive.

As well as the recognised kingdoms of nature there are others such as the elementals or nature spirits as well as *devas*, a Sanskrit term meaning 'shining ones'. These entities are better known in the West as the various classes of angels. Not all the hierarchies of the Earth exist in physical matter. Some exist solely in finer ethereal, astral or even mental matter and are difficult to perceive except for a few especially sensitive individuals.

All hierarchies are part of The Absolute or the Universal Consciousness. Like everything else they are distinct but inseparable aspects of The One. And yet all classes of life are always struggling for increased self-consciousness and an enhanced role in the grand evolutionary plan.

You could regard the overall hierarchical structure of The Earth as a large complex organisation or corporation with a layered management structure, many departments with different functions, responsibilities and grades and specialisations of workers as well as links to suppliers and customers.

There is a hidden hierarchy of highly advanced individuals sometimes called the inner government of the world which has the difficult task of overseeing progress in all kingdoms of nature to achieve the desired aims of planetary evolution. In their relationship with human beings their role is to influence our development without infringing all-important free will. They rarely, if ever, intervene directly. Human beings have to learn by their own mistakes. No one can do our learning for us either as a kingdom of nature or as individuals. We will deal with this more fully, later.

We might refer to The One Life or Universal Consciousness as the Cosmic Logos or Spirit. It energises the universe in three fundamental modes via a trinity of will, love-wisdom and active intelligence. This trinity is portrayed in Christianity as Father, Son and Holy Ghost. In Hinduism it is Brahma the creator, Vishnu the preserver and Shiva the destroyer. Many other religious traditions have their own variants of this trinity. We will deal with this in more depth in the section on **The Seven Rays**.

A key point to remember here is that all beings of whatever size, influence or complexity all live in the body of a greater being.

Closely associated with the Cosmic Logos are the seven Cosmic Planetary Logoi. All star systems in the universe which are centres of evolution belong to one of these seven and reflect their greater lives.

Nourishing us and directing activities in our own scheme is the Solar Logos or Spirit who also operates in this three-fold mode of will, love-wisdom and active intelligence. Working in tandem are the seven Planetary Logoi known in Hinduism as Lords of Creatures (*parajapatis*), in Christianity as the Seven Spirits Before The Throne of God and in Zoroastrianism as the seven Immortal Holy Ones (*amesha sapentas*). This high-ranking being is also known as The Silent Watcher or The Ancient of Days. The Planetary Logos also controls the various hierarchies of devas.

Below the Logos are the Four Kumaras or Lords of the Earth headed by Sanat Kumara or The Lord of The World. Each of the three lesser Kumaras are in charge of one of three major rays of aspect: will, love-wisdom and active intelligence. They are also known as Lords of the Flame or Buddhas of Activity.

Ray I (Will) is headed by The Manu otherwise known as Lord Vaivasvata; Ray II: (Love-Wisdom) The Boddishatva or Lord Maitreya and Ray III: (Active Intelligence) by The Mahachohan or Lord of Civilization.

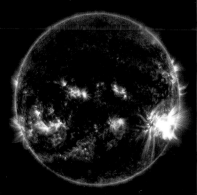

In rank below the kumaras are the Masters of Wisdom variously known as *chohans*, adepts and initiates. They are individuals who are masters of no one but themselves. Through their own efforts they have developed to a point where they are the vanguard of humanity. Individual masters – some in physical form – direct human activities. They preside over different fields of human activity and over different geographical areas.

Immediately in contact with the masters are various grades of initiates or *arhats* who have also advanced through various initiations. Below the initiates are their disciples, people who have chosen to accelerate their own spiritual development and are on the path of accelerated advancement. Probationers are the newcomers to that path.

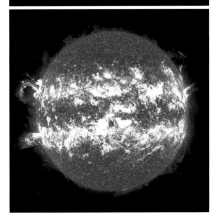

Making up the vast bulk of the world's population are individuals at various stages of psycho-spiritual development. In other words, us. And we represent a vast spectrum.

*Top: The Fairies of the Serpentine,* 1906, by English book illustrator, Arthur Rackham.
*Above: Iris* (detail), 1886, by English Victorian-era artist, John Atkinson Grimshaw.

## DEVAS AND ELEMENTALS

Deva is a Sanskrit word meaning celestial being or 'shining one'. They are equal in status to the kumaras but they are beings who are on a separate evolutionary scheme to that of the human, although they have passed through the human kingdom in previous cycles of evolution.

They no longer require physical form. They come in many different classes. Christianity calls them angels and archangels or thrones, dominions, principalities, virtues, powers, cherubim and seraphim. Other religions and spiritual traditions have their own names for them. The Planetary spirits are part of the deva kingdom, which is in advance of our own.

However, they are visible to a few people as vortices of energy or flashing trails of lights resembling wings. This is perhaps why they are likened to angels.

The most advanced devas work on the higher spiritual planes. Lesser ones (with a greater degree of form although mostly invisible) operate on the astral and etheric planes. Devas appearing as sylphs or cloud spirits may work under the command of other devas. Devas preside over trees, landscapes and bodies of water.

Our knowledge of the deva kingdom is extremely fragmentary. What we do know is that without them our world would not exist. The devas act as a kind of glue, holding the universe together. Paradoxically they seem to have no individuality and appear to be merged together in a group soul.

They are intimately involved in the creation of new human bodies and until a child is around seven years old will retain an elemental presence. Devas are also associated with healing. They may appear as guardian angels.

The devas control the elemental kingdoms and nature spirits. We may regard the devas as essentially the architects and the elementals as the builders. But the elementals are not part of the deva scheme. They are part of ours. Each species of plant has its own nature spirit.

Elementals and nature spirits belong to the three elemental kingdoms below the mineral. They build and preserve all the other four kingdoms of nature below the super-human.

They represent the different elements of air, earth, water and fire. In England we refer to these respectively as sylphs, gnomes, undines and salamanders. There are many local names for them. And different cultures have numerous different names for them - especially in Hinduism where there are literally hundreds of millions. Arab peoples called desert spirits djinns. The Irish have leprechauns or little people.

'The Elementals in the soul
of man are the products of
the action of the thought in
the individual mind of
man; the elemental forms
in the soul of the world
are the products of the
collective thoughts of all
beings.'

Franz Hartmann, *Magic White and Black*

The Norse have trolls.

Many elementals appear to have
a natural aversion to human beings
because of our apparently coarse and
disruptive vibrations. They are often
described as being extremely
mischievous, playing tricks on humans
and acting very much like naughty
children.

Belief in nature spirits was
extremely widespread throughout
the western world until the 18th
Century when science, rationalism
and industrialisation took over and
fundamentally changed people's attitude
to nature by concentrating people in
cities and divorcing them from the
natural world.

*Above left: The Fairy Feller's Masterstroke* (detail),
1885-64, by English artist, Richard Dadd.
*Left: Saint Giles - His Bells* by Victorian artist,
Charles Altamont Doyle and the father of Sir
Arthur Conan Doyle, creator of Sherlock Holmes.

## COSMIC & PLANETARY HIERARCHY

Throughout Theosophy and the Ageless Wisdom there are often many different names for the same being or concept – and this is particularly the case in describing the hierarchy of the world.

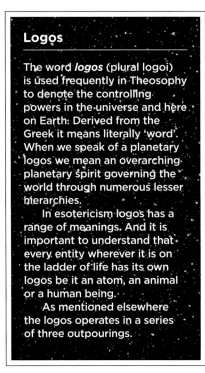

### Logos

The word *logos* (plural *logoi*) is used frequently in Theosophy to denote the controlling powers in the universe and here on Earth. Derived from the Greek it means literally 'word'. When we speak of a planetary logos we mean an overarching planetary spirit governing the world through numerous lesser hierarchies.

In esotericism logos has a range of meanings. And it is important to understand that every entity wherever it is on the ladder of life has its own logos be it an atom, an animal or a human being.

As mentioned elsewhere the logos operates in a series of three outpourings.

Universal Consciousness / Cosmic Logos

Solar Logos
A Trinity of Will, Love-Wisdom and Active Intelligence

Planetary Logos / The Silent Watcher / The Ancient of Days

Sanat Kumara /
Lord of The World

Devas or Archangels
equal in status but on a
separate evolutionary scheme

Three Kumaras / Lords of the Flame / Buddhas of Activity
each one in charge of three major rays of aspects:

Ray I
Will & Power
The Manu/Lord
Vaivasvata

Ray II
Love-Wisdom
The Boddishatva /
Lord Maitreya

Ray III
Active Intelligence
The Mahachohan or
Lord of Civilization

Various Masters of Wisdom / Chohans / Adepts

Initiates / Arhats

Disciples

Probationers

Average humanity

## THE MASTERS OF WISDOM

The Masters of Wisdom are referred to by a variety of names such as The Great White Brotherhood or Trans-Himalayan Brotherhood. They are called mahatmas (great soul in Sanskrit) or sometimes adepts. As key members of the inner government of the world they are said to play a pivotal behind-the-scenes role in guiding humanity.

A number of these masters have been named and identified. Two of them, Master Morya (known as M) and Koot Hoomi (sometimes Kuthumi and known as KH) based in the Northern India/Tibet were both in contact with HPB throughout her adult life. They are said to have played an important role in her writings, having a particular influence on *The Secret Doctrine*.

In the late 19th Century they also transmitted letters to a number of other leading Theosophists, especially Arthur Percy Sinnet, a prominent Indian newspaper editor of the day. They were also sent to members of Madame Blavatsky's family. They were written in distinctive red and blue scripts by the Masters M and KH. Interestingly the writing is not on the surface of the paper but actually embedded into it.

These documents were often delivered to their recipients in curious ways – for example, 'precipitated' out of thin air into a railway carriage. There are many hundreds of these fascinating letters, some of which are now collected in the British Library and are available in book form. Others are held elsewhere. They make absorbing reading.

Djwhal Khul (the Master DK) is sometimes known as the Tibetan Master and achieved this status some time after HPB's death. He directly inspired and even dictated most of the two dozen books by the prominent 20th Century esotericist Alice A Bailey.

Other members of this secret hierarchy include The Masters Jesus, Hilarion, Serapis and Jupiter, the English and Venetian Masters along with others. More of these masters are said to be coming into incarnation.

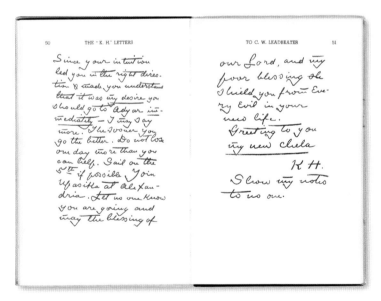

*Top:* A somewhat stylised depiction of Master Morya by David Anrias c1920s.
*Above:* The second letter from the Master K H to CW Leadbeater, received in 1888 and reproduced here in *The "K.H." Letters*.

*Below:* This picture was reputedly taken in Adyar in India in the 1880s. It shows Madame Blavatsky with the three masters with whom she worked to found the Theosophical Society. These individuals are shown as they appeared in the physical at that time – from left to right they are Master Kuthumi, Master Morya and the Comte St. Germain.

They are said to have been behind major world developments such as Theosophy but also the French and American Revolutions, spiritualism and reformist initiatives such as the labour and trade union movement.

Across the wide expanse of the internet there are countless references to ascended masters but as with all things it is best to be very open-minded about claims they make or those who channel their messages.

## Controversy

There has always been some doubt and scepticism about the existence of the masters even in Theosophical circles. While some believe they are a fiction, there are many who are convinced of their real and important role in world affairs.

Sceptics have always claimed that HPB wrote the letters herself, although examination of the letters and their means of delivery make this highly unlikely.

Matters are complicated by the many thousands of people who claim to channel the wisdom of exalted beings both from Earth and much further afield. Much of this material is likely to be bogus. Discernment is vital.

People often raise the question as to why these exalted spiritual statesman do not make themselves better known – especially at times when the world is in turmoil. The answer seems to be that these initiates and adepts work covertly with their assistants overshadowing certain promising individuals but not becoming directly involved since that would infringe both free will and the law of karma.

## The Initiations

Throughout the Ageless Wisdom tradition a lot is said about the question of spiritual initiation. Popularly this may be thought of as some kind of ceremonial graduation in a masonic or magic group in which the candidate wears robes and is conferred with titles. But it is much deeper than merely colourful ritual.

Initiation is derived from the Latin term 'to begin'. In esoteric terms it means embarking on a life with the deliberate intention of accelerating one's evolutionary process and rapidly expanding one's spiritual consciousness. It is sometimes described as 'entering the stream'. Nothing is left out – it is merely condensed into a shorter period. What might ordinarily take thousands or even millions of years is concentrated into a few lifetimes.

Anyone believing that embarking on advanced spiritual evolution is some sort of simple or soft option could not be more mistaken. Whenever an individual decides to embark upon what is commonly called The Path, things inevitably get much tougher. It is sometimes called The Path of Woe. Those choosing this shorter, steeper route frequently find the process very painful. Rather than life suddenly getting better it usually becomes extremely challenging.

Those choosing this route have to confront many unpleasant aspects of themselves – not least their karma and the way it presents itself in our lives. They also have to learn to carry on despite persistent failure.

Typically, there are said to be seven initiations in the Earth realm. These are sometimes described as stages in discipleship. And they involve increasingly closer contacts with members of the spiritual hierarchy of the Great White Brotherhood.

Initially, the would-be seeker or aspirant becomes a disciple or *chela*. The first three initiations involve the pupil first on the probationary path and then on the path of discipleship. The first three initiations also represent gaining control over the physical, astral and mental bodies respectively.

At the fourth initiation the pupil becomes an accepted disciple and at the fifth an adept or Master of Wisdom. It is said that it normally takes seven lives between the first and fourth initiations and a further seven lives between the fourth and fifth.

The sixth and seventh initiations elevate the individual to much higher status. However, since they are literally beyond human comprehension at this stage, little can be said about them.

Sometimes this series of initiations are compared to the life of Christ. The first is the birth, the second the baptism, the third the transfiguration, the fourth the crucifixion and the fifth the resurrection.

## THE SEVEN-FOLD HUMAN CONSTITUTION

We can separate human beings into different components in a number of ways. We can regard ourselves as a two-fold division of spirit and matter. Or we can look on ourselves as a trinity of body, emotions and mind.

We can also divide human beings into seven distinct aspects. Three of these 'bodies' are the permanent Ego which accompany us as an enduring 'soul' during our various incarnations in human bodies. The four transitory bodies make up the temporary Personality which is formed anew for each of our many lives on Earth. Who we are now has been shaped by our behaviour, conduct and actions in previous lives. Our future lives are being moulded by the life we are living now.

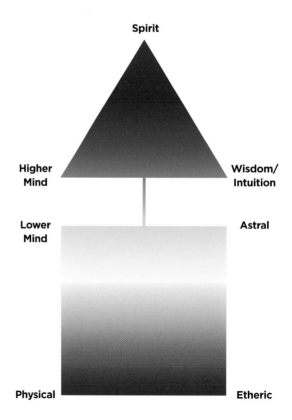

## SEVEN BODIES

The majority of people are only aware of their physical bodies, their emotions and their lower thoughts. Many do not imagine there is anything else.

We are all very aware of our physical bodies because of their ongoing needs and demands and the fact that they frequently go wrong. Science and medicine have taught us a lot about the physical working of our bodies. Many people devote much time to health and fitness. But as we shall see, although disease may occur on the physical plane its cause maybe on more subtle levels such as our emotions or thoughts.

Mirroring our physical bodies is an energising template most commonly known as the Etheric Double. This is essentially an animating principle for the physical frame, co-ordinating forces and energies to keep the body activated. It extends a little way outside the body and can be detected by some people as an aura. The etheric body also acts as a link between our astral and mental vehicles.

You can detect your own energy body by placing the flat palms of your hands about an inch apart. Many people can feel a pulsing or tingling feeling when they do this.

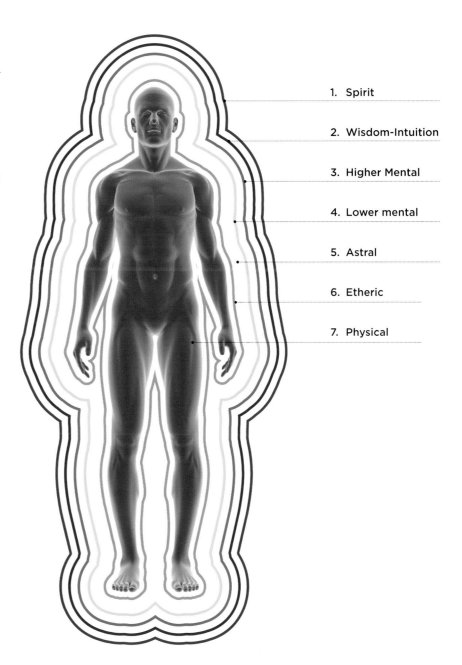

1.  Spirit

2.  Wisdom-Intuition

3.  Higher Mental

4.  Lower mental

5.  Astral

6.  Etheric

7.  Physical

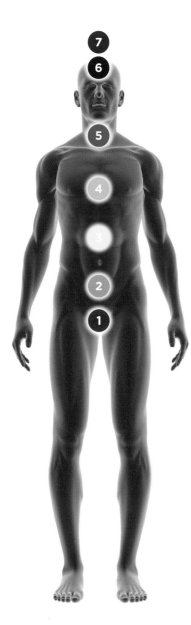

## CHAKRAS

The etheric body is home to a series of seven energy ports known as chakras (meaning 'wheel' or 'cycle' in Sanskrit). These seven centres or vortices are associated with different organs of the physical body, although the chakras themselves remain outside it. They are conductors of subtle energies known as ***prana*** and ***kundalini*** which interpenetrate the physical body and supply these vital forces.

There are seven different varieties of prana, each with a different function and correspond to one of the Rays. These vital energies keep us alive. Sometimes, chakras are considered to be counterparts to our endocrine glands. In the Eastern tradition they are often portrayed as lotus flowers with varying numbers of petals.

In recent years there has been much interest in the purpose and use of chakras in such areas as reiki healing. Much has been written on this subject and although an energy body has been central to Eastern medicine for millennia, it still remains on the fringe in the West.

**1 - Root:** Located at the base of the spine it is represented as having four petals. It is associated with the colour red and has an affinity to the earth element and is said to keep us grounded. It is connected with the elimination of waste solids from the body and linked to its more solid components such as bones, teeth and nails. It is also connected to the 'fight or flight' response, survival and the sense of smell. It governs mental stability, emotional sensuality and spiritual security.

**2 - Sacral:** This six-petal white chakra is found at the sacrum of the spine. It is linked to water and both fluid elimination from the body and the balance of fluids within it. This chakra is connected to the testes, ovaries, sexual activity and reproduction. It is associated with the sense of taste and also influences movement, athletics and dance. It is also connected to violence, relationships, addictions and emotional needs as well as creativity, enthusiasm and joy.

**3 - Solar Plexus:** Linked to the element fire, it is responsible for the expansive aspects of our nature. Portrayed as yellow with ten petals this chakra is concerned with maintaining the equilibrium of the digestive system. Associated with the sense of sight, it influences the way we see things – especially the intensity of colour (depending on our mood). It controls fear, anxiety and the transition from simple to complex emotions. It governs personal power and spiritual growth.

**4 - Heart:** Situated at the level of the breastbone this chakra is linked to air and matters of the heart such as love, gentleness and compassion but also lightness and ease of mobility. It is associated with the sense of touch and with sympathetically reaching out to others. Represented as green or pink, it is linked to the immune system and also the circulation. It deals with compassion, complex emotions, equilibrium, unconditional love and tenderness as well as spiritual devotion.

**5 - Throat:** With sixteen blue or turquoise petals this chakra governs speech and nourishing of the body through eating, drinking and breathing. As well as providing energy for vital functions it is also the key link between the lower four and higher three chakras. It is linked to the thyroid gland which controls growth and maturation. It governs emotional independence, fluent thought and spiritual security.

**6 - Brow:** Situated next to the pituitary gland in the centre of the brow, this chakra is the major controller of the body's glands. It is also known as the *ajna* or third eye centre. Represented as indigo or deep blue with 96 petals, this is the location of the mind and where mental activity and thought are concentrated but this centre is also linked to psychic activity. Its role is to balance the higher and lower selves but it is also connected to visual consciousness and intuition.

**7 - Crown:** Located on top of the head and linked to the pineal gland deep within the brain, it is the 960- or more commonly thousand-petal lotus. In the Ageless Wisdom teachings the pineal gland was formerly used for psychic communication before the development of speech. Although this faculty has atrophied, significant numbers of people still retain some of this ability. Theosophy stresses that the pineal gland is associated with the unfoldment of higher psychic faculties via advanced spiritual development. This is the point at which the soul departs after 'death'.

The four lower chakras are connected with the lower four bodies of the transient Personality while the three higher are linked to our three-fold permanent reincarnating Individuality.

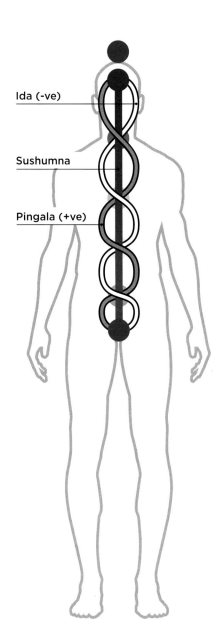

Ida (-ve)

Sushumna

Pingala (+ve)

The actual physical infrastructure used to transmit these energies involves three main connections known as *nadis* (in Sanskrit 'tubular vessel'). The central tube or *sushumna* runs down the spinal cord with two other channels spiralling around it in a figure-of-eight configuration. The left side has the negative, feminine based *ida* while on the right is the positive, masculine *pingala*. (Some versions of the Ageless Wisdom reverse this positioning.)

These twin channels vitalise each chakra magnetically inducing them to rotate or vibrate at different rates. Each of these chakras has a higher rate of vibration than the one below it so that the crown chakra has the highest rate of all.

There is an additional ultra-powerful spiritual force at the base of the spine known as *kundalini*. We will discuss the dangers of misusing this extremely powerful and dangerous energy later. This force awakens and becomes more potent as individuals develop spiritually. There is speculation that because of their importance in the far future human beings may develop double spinal cords.

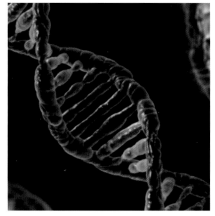

*Above left:* This ancient symbol of two serpents curled in a spiral around a central rod is known as the Caduceus, which represents growth from lowest material levels to the spiritual realms. It is also known as the Rod of Hermes. In the modern age it has been adopted as a worldwide symbol of the medical profession. Interestingly, it corresponds closely to the double-helix structure of DNA first identified in the 1950s *(above right)*.

## OTHER REALMS

Over the past few decades there has been increasing awareness of the astral world and the fact that humans have astral bodies. The astral realm is made of matter much finer than the physical. It is said to extend from some way inside the earth to almost as far as the moon. The astral realm is the word of desire and emotion. We all travel there every night when we sleep and dream. We visit this realm (more accurately a state of consciousness rather than a place) for a time after we die. Some people are able to deliberately access the astral plane, which we will describe later.

Over millions of years human beings have increasingly developed intellect, thought and the power of reason. We have learned how to use our minds creatively – and also very destructively. It is important to remember that the mind is more than just the brain. It extends far beyond it. The brain is just the processor on the physical plane – essential but not exclusive.

In reality we do not have a single unified mind. It is divided into two distinct parts – the lower and the higher. The lower is what is called the concrete mind which dwells on mundane matters and everyday concerns. It is very often ruled and driven by the emotions coming from our astral bodies it is sometimes called the 'desire mind'. (In Sanskrit *kama* means desire and *manas* means mind. Do not confuse kama with karma, The Law of Cause and Effect.)

The higher mind is concerned with more elevated concepts such as creative activities, philosophising, appreciating art, beauty and culture. It is sometimes called the causal body. This becomes a sub-conscious storehouse of our experience gathered over many different lives. We can regard it as an invisible hard drive containing a record of everything we have ever done, thought or felt.

So the mind can be regarded as having seven segments or sub-planes – three making up the higher mind and four lower making up the lower concrete one. Our lower minds cease at the time of physical death but our higher minds are recycled as part of our permanent Ego which reincarnates.

Also permanent and part of our Egos are two other higher principles. Above the higher mind is the world of wisdom and intuition (*buddhi*). This is a faculty latent in many people but as we evolve this will become part of our standard apparatus of perception along with our physical senses. Human beings have many other capacities, capabilities and potential faculties which currently remain dormant and which will unfold in the future depending on individual self-effort and attainment.

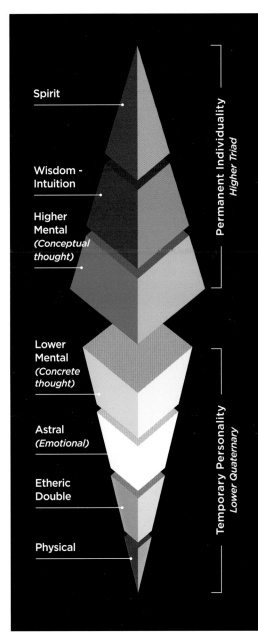

Spirit

Wisdom - Intuition

Higher Mental *(Conceptual thought)*

Permanent Individuality *Higher Triad*

Lower Mental *(Concrete thought)*

Astral *(Emotional)*

Etheric Double

Physical

Temporary Personality *Lower Quaternary*

## The rainbow bridge

Between our temporary Personalities and permanent Egos is a gulf to which there is a potential link between our lower and higher mental bodies. We have to work to develop this bridge through increasing self-awareness, higher conduct, meditation and other techniques. This is often called the 'rainbow bridge' (in Sanskrit *antahkarana*).

At the summit of our bodies is our spirit (*atma*) – our direct contact with the refined world of spirit.

Often these bodies are portrayed as sitting on top of one another like rock strata or a layer-cake with the physical at the centre and the spiritual at the outer fringes. It is important to know that these bodies are in fact intermingled.

Our five physical senses have gradually unfolded at the rate of one per development group, or Root Race – beginning with hearing. (We will deal with Root Races shortly). But as mentioned earlier, these senses are extremely limited. For example, we can see on the physical spectrum only between infra-red and ultra-violet. X-rays, microwaves and radio waves are entirely invisible to us.

To repeat: our lowest four bodies, the physical, etheric, astral and lower mind make up what is called our Personality and are newly created for each incarnation. They are impermanent and 'die' with the physical body.

Our three higher bodies, the higher mental, wisdom-intuition and spirit form our permanent Individuality or Ego which we carry from life to life. These are evolving but indestructible principles. This is a vitally important idea at the very core of Theosophy - hence this repetition

'Without going outside, you may know the whole world.
Without looking through the window, you may see the ways of heaven.
The farther you go, the less you know.
Thus the sage knows without travelling;
He sees without looking;
He works without doing.'

*Lao Tzu,* Tao Te Ching

## AURAS

Everyone is familiar with the term but there are many different definitions of what it is. We speak of people's auras when in fact most people cannot physically see them (although some sensitive people can). We detect them through our other invisible bodies.

Auras are egg-shaped, made up of our thoughts and emotions and extend some way from our bodies. Our auras intermingle with those of others. This is one explanation for why we feel instantly repelled or attracted by certain people. We affect others and we ourselves are affected by this mixing of emotional and mental energies. Sometimes we refer to this as people emitting good or bad 'vibes'. Many animals and young children are particularly sensitive to other people's auras either positively or negatively.

In collective situations with gatherings of people such as sports, musical and political events or religious meetings the mixture of auras produces a collective consciousness – often for the worse. Hundreds or thousands of people can be turned into a screeching, destructive mob by one or more individuals. Hysteria is easy to achieve – especially today.

*Below:* These illustrations, produced from clairvoyant observations of auras by Charles Leadbeater, show the various effects on the aura by differing emotions. They are snapshots of our astral bodies. Anger shows as red, fear as grey, brown as depression and mauve as spirituality.

**1. Fear** This shows how the astral body of an individual reacts to sudden shock or terror. It is suffused by a grey mist with sharp jagged lines of the same colour.

**2: Calm and scientific** This is the aura of someone with a relaxed, inquiring mind. Well-developed intelligence is shown by the golden yellow in the area of the head while the orange cone indicates pride and ambition. The ordered mind is shown by the regular bands of colour.

**3. Irritation** Outbursts of temper at the frustrations of life are indicated by the scarlet specks, some of which are directed outwards towards the source of irritation.

**4. Anger** The aura is dominated by thick black swirls as the individual is consumed by extreme anger. Fiery red slashes are like piercing the astral bodies of others with arrows.

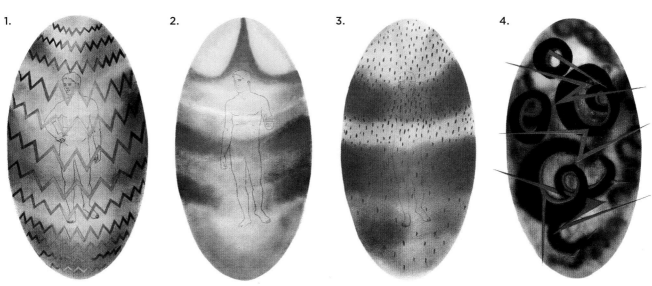

1.        2.        3.        4.

## Controversy

There are a number of different classifications of the seven human bodies or vehicles. This has been an ongoing source of discord especially in the Theosophical movement for more than a century. The difficulty arose when Annie Besant *(below)*, the second president of the Theosophical Society amended these classifications from those set out by HPB. The term 'astral' was given a different meaning from that outlined by Blavatsky.

The important thing to recognise here is that we are far more than our physical frames – or even our emotions and minds. We have both temporary and permanent bodies.

# MONAD

This is a widely-used occult term signifying a permanent fragment of The One or The Absolute – the ultimate elements of the universe. A monad is an indivisible and eternal spiritual entity or life-atom – and a centre of consciousness and self-consciousness. It has been described as humans' only immortal and eternal principle.

It can be looked on as a seed which has the ultimate capacity to produce numerous other seeds. Monads therefore generate hosts of other living entities. Each entity in every kingdom has a monad, so there are mineral, animal and vegetable, as well as human monads, at different stages of evolution. Human monads have passed through all the lower kingdoms on their journey.

Monads originally passed through one of the seven planetary logoi. They are overshadowed and dominated by the characteristics of the ray of that logos.

The term *monadic essence* is often used and this can be regarded as the energy behind evolution. This is the life of the second logos on the four highest planes of the solar system. It descends and re-ascends at the end of each cycle of development.

# 3. THE HUMAN PROJECT

## SEVEN ROOT RACES

Human evolution began in the Paleozoic era up to 150 million years ago and not as science insists a mere two million years ago. Human beings in a form we might vaguely recognise have been on Earth for some 18.7 million years. Earlier, non-physical human prototypes may go back much further – long before the extinction of the dinosaurs. In their early stages of development they bore no resemblance physically, emotionally or mentally to modern humans.

Prior to that human development was confined to another planetary scheme of evolution centred on our moon.

Although the Ageless Wisdom offers an expansive evolutionary blueprint, where it fundamentally departs from Darwinian and modern concepts of evolution is that it is quite clear: *man did NOT develop from the apes.* The opposite is true.

With human development – as in all other schemes of evolution – the seven-fold principle is the template. Human evolution in this cycle involves our progressing through seven key development groups known as Root Races, each of which lasts for around 8.5 million years. Each of these is divided into seven sub-races which last around 1.25 million years. Each sub-race is further divided into branch-races and further divisions.

Races rise and fall along with the civilizations they create and destroy. No human empire can ever be immortal. Periods of progress and enlightenment are succeeded by phases of decadence and decay followed by dark ages of ignorance and repression. But there is always a renaissance – often concentrated in a single locality – and this eventually gains much wider influence. We have currently progressed to the fifth sub-race of the fifth Root Race and so we are more than halfway through the present cycle.

At some point each Root Race splits. In 16,000 to 20,000 years' time it is said that the present Aryan Race will divide in the same way that previous Root Races

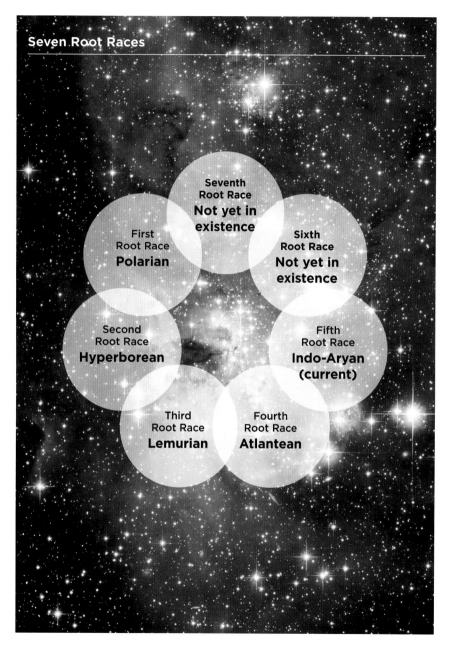

**Seven Root Races**

Seventh Root Race
**Not yet in existence**

First Root Race
**Polarian**

Sixth Root Race
**Not yet in existence**

Second Root Race
**Hyperborean**

Fifth Root Race
**Indo-Aryan (current)**

Third Root Race
**Lemurian**

Fourth Root Race
**Atlantean**

have done. Future races will follow the same pattern.

It is important to note that both Races and sub-races overlap one another to a considerable degree and are not end-on. Each one of us is likely to have incarnated a number of times in different family- or nation-branches of a particular sub-race.

We can view these Root Races, sub-races and the further divisions as development groups of humanity. Each one offers its own unique conditions and learning experiences. Every one of us has progressed through these groupings as we have incarnated in numerous lives spanning millions of years. And we will continue our onward – and infinite journey – through the coming sub-races and Root Races before the cycle reaches the seventh sub-race of the Seventh Root Race. At that stage this part of the human project will be complete and many of us will progress to those kingdoms more elevated than the human.

It is interesting to speculate where humanity's future lies when the Earth project is finally over. However, given that the time-spans involved are so gigantic and that our own consciousness has a considerable way to unfold, speculation must remain exactly that.

## THE FIRST ROOT RACE

Our knowledge of the First Root Race, The Polarian is extremely limited. It came into existence 130-150 million years ago. What we know is that they were 'self-born' with very etherealised and astralised rather than physical bodies. With no self-consciousness they lived for millions of years on the so-called White Continent or the Imperishable Sacred Land.

This marked the start of what is called the Fourth Round of the Earth's development. Evolved spirits from a previous evolutionary scheme, the Moon Chain, arrived and embodied in these 'mindless' forms in an attempt to stimulate them from their stagnant state. They were known as Lords of the Moon or *Lunar Pitris*. Progress remained unimpressively slow.

Members of the First Root Race, sometimes known as The Shadow Race, resembled huge bags of translucent, finer than physical matter, perhaps 120 feet tall. They reproduced by fission – splitting in two as amoeba do. They developed the first of our five physical senses, hearing. Over vast periods of time the earth elementals created more solid shells for these proto-humans. This was the beginning of our having physical bodies.

As is the case with the transition from one Root Race to the next, there were huge changes to the surface of the Earth with landmasses vanishing and new ones appearing to form the continents where the evolution of that race would take place.

## THE SECOND ROOT RACE

The Second Race or The Hyperborean originated 25-30million years ago. These early humans were also gigantic compared to modern man – about 60 feet tall. Like their forebears they were also single sex – or more accurately sexless. They occupied an area which is now covered by Northern Asia and Greenland. But in those days this region was no icy waste but had a tropical climate because of a different alignment of the Earth's axis.

They were also known as the 'sweat-born' because they reproduced by a process of 'budding', exuding fluids which coalesced into eggs and hatched as offspring. They were initially boneless but had a primitive form of language and they developed the second of our senses, touch. They also evolved a chant-like sound language consisting only of vowels. Over a long period of time, as they progressed through the seven sub-races, they developed skin and rudimentary bone structures. Being only partly physical there was no death as we understand it now. It was more a process of constant recycling and renewal.

This process bubbled on uninterrupted in the terrestrial test-tube for millennia with imperceptibly slow progress. Then, after this languorous slow-burn of a development, humanity gradually began to shake itself awake. There were cataclysmic changes not only to the Earth itself but also to its human inhabitants in order to clear the way for the next development group. Destruction always precedes creation and further stages of evolution.

As new lands formed, the vanguard of the humanity of that time reached a crucial tipping point where a new cycle of advancement bloomed – eventually. But it was not without further outside intervention.

## THE THIRD ROOT RACE

The Third Root Race, The Lemurian, saw the beginnings of the human race as we know it and members of this race developed physical characteristics and a bone structure. This was where our development began to dramatically accelerate – especially the evolution of human knowledge. From the start of the race to its end there were phenomenal developments with humans at the start of the race bearing no resemblance at all to those at the end of it.

These humans were still enormous and began to evolve sight, initially through a single eye. This is where we get myths of the cyclops and the Titans of ancient Greece. And giants are found in the legends and folklore from cultures all around the world. The race acquired a rudimentary sense of sight. First they developed two additional eyes while the central one began to atrophy. This is the location in the centre of the forehead that we now refer to as the Third Eye.

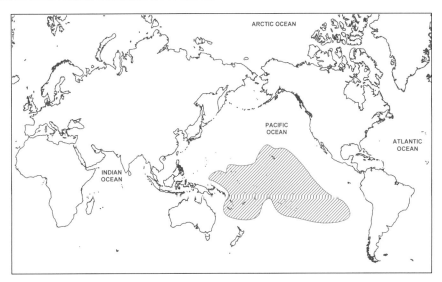

In the early stages of the race they were still sweat-born but developed other means of reproduction. Dual sexuality emerged and the race became hermaphrodites (both sexes in one). By the mid-point of the race two sexes had developed and reproduction as we know it had begun.

This happened 18.7 million years ago and represents what Christians call 'The Fall' into generation and corresponds to the creation of Adam and Eve in The Garden of Eden.

The continent of Lemuria was truly vast extending from the southern tip of Africa to Scandinavia and across the Indian Ocean encompassing Australia and across the Pacific Ocean as far as the Californian coast. To the south it stretched as far as Antarctica.

However, attempts to improve consciousness had proved less than successful.

*Above:* Easter Island (1880), a fragment of Lemuria?

## 'Sins of the mindless'

During the Third Root Race some Lemurians mated with animals and the result was a sub-race of dumb ape-like but semi-human monstrosities, the distant progenitors of today's anthropoid apes such as the orang-utang, chimpanzee, gorilla and baboon.

*The Ageless Wisdom is quite clear that these apes descended from man and NOT that man descended from the apes. This is diametrically opposed to modern Darwinian-inspired evolutionary beliefs.*

Later, members of the third or fourth sub-race of the Atlantean period re-committed this inter-species pairing with some males mating with dumb female monsters left over from the mid-Lemurian period. These interactions were described as 'sins of the mindless' by Blavatsky in *The Secret Doctrine.*

Unlike most of the Lemurian monsters, these did not die out but mutated into the ancestors of our modern day anthropoids.

Humans remained dumb and animal-like. Advanced beings from another system again intervened under the Law of Compassion to assist the Lemurians' stalled evolution.

The Lords of the Flame from Venus, also known as *Manasaputras* or Sons of Mind (and literally dozens of other names) arrived to awaken the mental principle in man, vital to all future development of the human species. This stimulating contact did not bear immediate fruit. Eventually, it did.

The Lemurians developed an extensive civilization with large buildings and a knowledge of metals. As well as architecture they cultivated the arts, sciences, astronomy and mathematics. But this took many hundreds of years after their psychological transformation. The first cities appeared in what is now Madagascar.

Eventually Lemuria underwent a catastrophic collapse with the continent sinking into the oceans leaving only remnants such as Easter Island, Sri Lanka and other tiny fragments of land.

At present we do not have sufficient information to specifically identify the sub-races of the first three Root Races.

## THE FOURTH ROOT RACE

The Fourth Root Race, the Atlantean began to emerge from around the mid-point of the Third Race around 10-12 million years ago and was centred on a group of Northern Lemurians based in what is now the mid-Atlantic. They continued with two sexes and physicalised bodies. Although still huge compared to modern man, their stature progressively decreased.

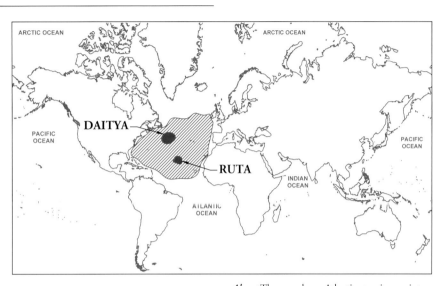

They developed the fourth sense of taste along with the full sense of sight via two eyes. By the middle point of the Atlantean Root Race – around two million years ago – human beings had developed physically into how they are today. Crucially, this was when speech was fully developed. Surprising as it may seem there had been no need for language before this since communication was via a form of thought-transference.

These events happened during the fourth sub-race – coinciding with the lowest point of the arc of involutionary descent. It also marked the point of divergence between the animal and human kingdoms. From that point it was no longer possible for any animal monad to individualise into the human kingdom. (It will no longer be possible for animals to join the human kingdom until the next round, the fifth. This is explained in more detail later.)

All this coincided with a great intellectual leap forward. The Atlantean continent, which was the residue of the Lemurian super-continent, spanned the Atlantic Ocean from Canada to the Scilly Isles in the north and from Brazil to West Africa in the south. Throughout its long history Atlantis underwent a series of cataclysms.

A series of cataclysms re-shaped the continent over hundreds of thousands of years, eventually leaving two islands, Ruta in the south and Daitya in the north. Located in the Gulf of Mexico, Ruta included parts of Bolivia, Peru, Central America and Mexico. Daitya, in the northern Atlantic, incorporated the Canary, Madeira and Azores island chains as well as North Africa, the Iberian Peninsular,

*Above:* The map shows Atlantis at various points in its history with the blue area showing it at its most extensive. Various cataclysms finally reduced it to two islands and finally a single landmass.
*Below:* The Atlantean civilization developed sophisticated technologies, including flying machines known as vimanas. However, their attempts to manipulate the laws of nature may have precipitated their own downfall.

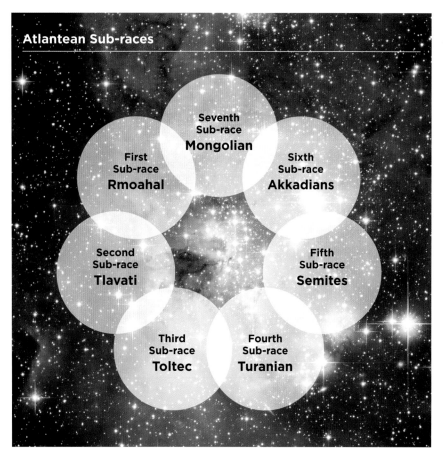

**Atlantean Sub-races**

Seventh
Sub-race
**Mongolian**

First
Sub-race
**Rmoahal**

Sixth
Sub-race
**Akkadians**

Second
Sub-race
**Tlavati**

Fifth
Sub-race
**Semites**

Third
Sub-race
**Toltec**

Fourth
Sub-race
**Turanian**

France Italy and Switzerland. Further cataclysms around 1.5 million years ago submerged Ruta while Daitya survived until about 270,000 years ago.

Beginning about 850,000 years ago and lasting for 150,000 years most of the islanders perished in various disasters. Throughout this entire period there were migrations to other parts of the world. Finally Atlantis was reduced to a single island encompassing the Canaries and the Azores and called Poseidonis, which disappeared in a final cataclysm around 12,000 years ago.

Atlantean civilization reached a high degree of sophistication and in many ways bore some of the hallmarks of 21st Century living. They were a technologically advanced race with flying machines, canal systems, great architecture and knowledge of metals. But they became corrupt and materialistic. And eventually they were destroyed by black magic.

Atlantean society divided into two groups: the black magicians known as the Lords or the Dark Face and their white counterparts called Lords of the Dazzling Face. The dark lords operated on the evil Left Hand Path precipitating a series crisis which affected the elemental forces of the planet.

They tried to control subterranean elemental spirits and harness the powers of the sun showing the same kind of arrogance that some scientists do today, believing they could subjugate nature to their will. Some of the white magicians understood that they had reached a point of no return and that nature would produce a violent sympathetic reaction. Many planned their exodus.

These events are recalled in Christianity as The Deluge or The Flood.

## THE FIFTH ROOT RACE

The current Fifth Root Race, the Indo Aryan, began to emerge in Central Asia about a million years ago, although the seeds of this development group extend back into Atlantean times. Its emergence and development was influenced by the mass migrations from Atlantis during the various phases of its destruction.

The First and Second Root Races, in which we developed sensation and activity, have now died out completely. The Third Root Race, which saw the emergence of emotion, is in the process of dying out. Members of the Fourth Root Race remain among us. The evolutionary process works on the basis that the level reached by the leading race or individuals is communicated to all.

The Fifth Root Race is concerned with the development of consciousness and especially social organisation. It involves developing minds which can synthesise and co-operate.

Compared to previous cycles we can be more precise about how the Fifth Root Race has developed – especially in its later stages. Our knowledge of history and increasingly sophisticated archaeological techniques give us many more specific details. There is no doubt that The Renaissance, the Enlightenment and then the Scientific, Industrial and so-called Communications and Information Revolutions have all rapidly increased the expansion of human's mental capacities – at least in the lower concrete mind. This has been the chief achievement of the present stage of development. The recognition of man's spiritual nature has not been so comprehensive or rapid. The increased intermingling of cultures over the past 500 years especially has been an accelerant to our mental evolution. Travel and wider horizons truly have broadened our minds.

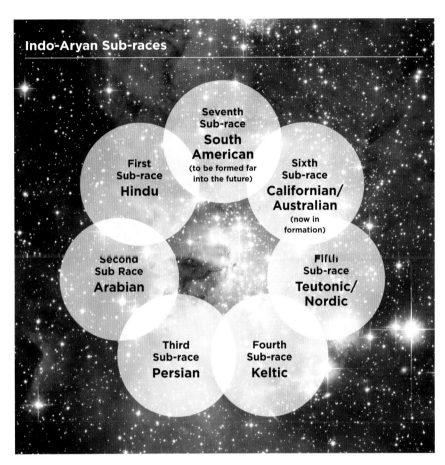

**Indo-Aryan Sub-races**

First Sub-race
**Hindu**

Seventh Sub-race
**South American**
(to be formed far into the future)

Sixth Sub-race
**Californian/ Australian**
(now in formation)

Second Sub Race
**Arabian**

Fifth Sub-race
**Teutonic/ Nordic**

Third Sub-race
**Persian**

Fourth Sub-race
**Keltic**

*Note:* As in many aspects of the Ageless Wisdom there are many variations in the names given to the races. It should be noted that the words 'Aryan' and 'Teutonic' have nothing whatsoever to do with Nazi or similar concepts of racial purity or superiority.

## Race Rulers

Each race has a guiding spirit known as a *Manu* who oversees such things as physical development and the migrations of people. There is also a supreme spiritual teacher known as the *Bodhisattva* who directs intellectual development and emotional intelligence via religions, arts and sciences.

## THE FIRST SUB-RACE: HINDU

This first group, the Hindu, was formed by fleeing white Atlantean magicians in Northern Asia in the areas now covered by the Gobi Desert in Mongolia and Afghanistan. It was separated from Atlantis but co-existed with it for around 200,000 years. There is always such an overlap between these races with one forming while the other gradually recedes.

Over time the sub-race emigrated south and settled in the Indus Valley – hence its name Hindu (which means of the Indus). This occurred around 12,000 years ago. It further developed language and writing. From this developed the rich diversity of Indian culture and social organisation, much of which remains today despite India's modernisation and industrialisation.

The early roots of Hinduism are seen in the literature of the *Vedas* and the *Upanishads*. This was followed much later by Buddhism.

*Left:* Vrishaketu and Bhima Fighting Yavanatha. A scene from the Story of Babhruvahana, folio from a Mahabharata, circa 1850.

## THE SECOND SUB-RACE: ARABIAN

The second sub-race was centred in Arabia and Egypt. Up to 4,000 BC immigrants from Western Asia brought a higher culture which transformed society and produced the great Egyptian civilization. This was influenced by ideas developed during the first sub-race. This was a land of many gods but governed by a supreme deity Amen-Ra (The Sun God) and subject to absolute rule by their temporal representative the Pharaoh. He represented absolute power.

Hidden knowledge was taught to initiates in the various Mystery Schools. Ritual, art and architecture reached new heights along with the sophisticated social system required to build its pyramids, gigantic temples and other grandiose monuments.

These were both a spiritual and practical people. However, for most people the mind had still not developed objective abilities. Therefore, they regarded external events as due to divine intervention and accepted them unquestioningly.

The modern descendants of this sub-race are the Arabs of North Africa and the Middle East, who are mainly Muslim.

*Above:* Egyptian hunting in the marshes. *Right:* The hieroglyphics alphabet is made up of drawings representing the sound of the letter.

## THE THIRD SUB-RACE: PERSIAN

Like most of the sub-races of the Fifth Race, the third sub-race, the Iranian or Persian, was also centred in the Near and Middle East from the Aegean Sea to Afghanistan. This group included the empires built by the Hittites, Babylonians, Persians and Assyrians.

In this grouping the social mind tended to express itself through emotion. The governments of these groups underwent a number of distinct changes corresponding to changes in consciousness. The early tribal kings squabbled for power and supremacy amongst themselves. An emperor took over and this developed into a monarchy in which kings ruled in consultation with their nobles.

A key development was the emergence of Zoroastrianism, the religion in which the deity is represented by the purifying power of fire.

The third sub-race distinguished itself through its artistic achievement such as decorative architecture, metalwork, ceramics and luxury textiles. Much of this reflected religious symbolism and royal power. Poetry and song were central to the peoples' lives. Science also emerged in the form of astronomy and astrology but these were sacred rather than cold and rational and practised solely by the all-powerful priesthood, the magi.

It is from the Babylonians that we get our seven day week and an hour of 60 minutes. Interestingly there are many common elements in the religion and art of the Iranians and the Middle Ages in Europe.

*Left:* Assyrian relief carvings. *Above:* Relief moulding of the lion of Babylon, originally from the Processional Way in Babylon.

## THE FOURTH SUB-RACE: KELTIC

The Keltic sub-race was divided into two distinct sub-groups, the Alpine and Mediterranean, who migrated to Europe from Asia Minor around 5,000 BC. The Alpine group settled in mainland Europe from Russia to France and became the rump of the continent's current population. The others, including Sumerians, Cretans, members of the great Greek and Roman civilizations as well as Iberians settled along the Mediterranean coastal areas.

These peoples developed the beginnings of an analytical mind but also a love of beauty. Geometry and logic were their specialities. Although logic ruled the style of government, the monarchs remained absolute.

Language developed to give clear and unambiguous expression to this new analytical way of thinking as shown in Latin and Greek.

An analysis of the various nations of this sub-race illustrates how it evolved psychologically through its various phases. The first national groups developed sensation and activity while the Greeks were fundamentally emotional. The later analytical mind of the Romans flourished into the synthesising mind of nations such as Italy, France and Spain.

The Greeks' love of activity, form and beauty gave way to the lower concrete and analytical mind of the Romans typified by its practical use of scientific discovery. The later Latin nations further fused and developed these faculties.

*Right:* Athenian terracotta column-krater (bowl for mixing wine and water). *Far right:* Roman mosaic, Palazzo Massimo, Rome.

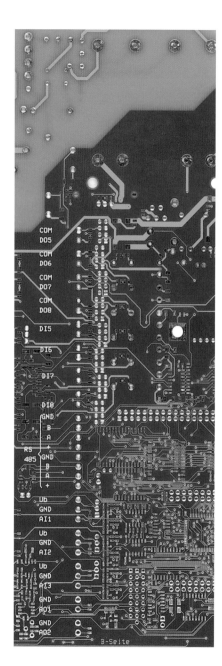

## THE FIFTH SUB-RACE: TEUTONIC/NORDIC

The chief characteristic of the fifth sub-race is the development of what might be called social consciousness and the synthesising mind. This group first emerged in Europe during the Roman Empire but its influence did not begin until the empire's break-up in the 5th Century.

It consists of various groups each presiding over a period of development. In the first wave, the Slavs, Central Europeans and Russians developed perception while in the second Prussians and neighbouring groups enforced top-down dominance via imperial command. The third group of Germans and Austrians elevated the arts especially music while the fourth group, the Dutch developed further mental analytical capabilities, high organisational skills and an efficient social system. The fifth sub-race consisting of Britain and Scandinavia is the current focal point for development, although its influence will eventually wane.

The chief mission faced by all the sub-races of the Fifth Root Race has been focused on developing and refining mental capabilities as well as preparing for new forms of consciousness. The current ubiquitous reliance on and addiction to technological progress at any price will undoubtedly have long-term consequences.

*Left:* Printed circuit board – a highly potent symbol of the concrete mind. ***Above:*** Kuala Lumpur, Malaysia. The 'synthesising' consciousness of the fifth sub-race has produced our current highly technological, inter-connected and global civilisation – with all its advantages, complexities and conflicts.

## THE SIXTH AND SEVENTH ROOT RACES

The Fifth Root Race still has a long way to run before the eventual emergence of the Sixth and Seventh Root Races at some point far into the future. The sixth sub-race of our current Fifth Root Race is already developing in The West Coast of the United States, as well as in South Africa and Australia. It means the vanguard of the next developmental stage for humanity are already walking among us.

It will be some centuries before this group begins to have an influence as the new guiding force within the human race. This sixth sub-race will form the template for the Sixth Root Race. Before that occurs, around 25,000 years from now, the seeds of the seventh sub-race will emerge in South America.

The means of reproduction will also change. In the Sixth Root Race hermaphroditism will reappear and we shall reproduce using a combination of will and imagination in a process sometimes known as *kriashakti*. This will occur passively at first and then actively in the Seventh Root Race. Human bodies will also change, becoming smaller and softer and finally ethereal and translucent.

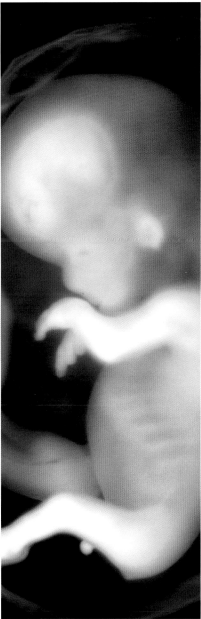

## Types of Karma

Karma is not there to crush us. As a rule, we do not begin to deal with particular karma and attempt to neutralise it until we are equipped mentally, emotionally and physically to do so.

We can identify three basic sub-categories of karma. Firstly, there is the karma we have built up but which has not yet produced any effects in our lives because of other karmic causes.

Secondly, there is the karma we are building up in this life and which will be burned off in a future life when the circumstances are appropriate.

Thirdly, there is the karma which is impacting on our current lives which was set up in previous incarnations.

' Suffering is a wonderful teacher – suffering is most people's only spiritual teacher.'

Eckhart Tolle

## KARMA & REINCARNATION

Theosophy refutes the normal view of death and its connotations of extinction and annihilation. It calls for a radical rethink and reinterpretation of the death of the physical body. In the West many, mainly religious people believe in the survival of the 'soul' or 'spirit' after death but far fewer believe that it returns to occupy another body in a future life on Earth.

Karma or the Law of Cause and Effect is a powerful idea which is recognised almost universally but is often grossly misunderstood and over-simplified. Karma only makes any real sense when we link it with the notion of reincarnation. It provides a continuum shaping our many different lives in human bodies. It is an immutable law of the universe. It cannot be evaded. It is not optional.

Although it can be delayed until the time is right, sooner or later we have to face our karma and deal with it. The word karma is derived from the Sanskrit word *kri* which means to make or do. So it means action. It is the combined result of all our thoughts, words and deeds. To quote a modern phrase: '*What goes around, comes around.*'

Nothing happens in the universe without a cause – even if we cannot detect it. It is absurd to believe that an event happens without something prompting it. In this sense when we use words like 'accident', 'coincidence' or 'luck' they are rather misleading terms.

The Law of Karma and Reincarnation is often called the law of laws. It is also often referred to as The Cycle of Necessity and sometimes The Law of Opportunity. It is perhaps the most important of all the ideas in this book.

Neither good nor bad, karma is a re-balancing law to restore the harmony and equilibrium which has been disrupted by our behaviour. We speak of good and bad karma, although really there is no such thing. We may regard events or circumstances as punishment or reward but this is very subjective. For example, if we are born into poor and miserable circumstances it may be regarded as our just desserts for previous misdeeds. But perhaps in a previous life we had an over-abundance of wealth and luxury which had somehow restricted our progress. In our current life our 'soul purpose' could be to counteract the previous material comforts and learn new lessons.

Karma only affects the lower parts of our make-up. Our immortal spiritual natures never fall victim to karma. Our karma is not just individual but also collective. We are all subject to the karma of the world itself, to a nation, town, family or organisation. Because of our associations we are bound up in that group karma which consists of all the thoughts, words and deeds of every individual who has ever been part of that group.

'...the final goal cannot be reached in any way but through life experiences, and the bulk of these consist in pain and suffering.'

H P Blavatsky, *The Key to Theosophy*

Disentangling what is personal and what is collective karma is therefore extraordinarily difficult if not impossible for most people at their present stage of development.

And since most of us have little or no knowledge of past lives, we have no idea of the source of our present fortune or misery. It may even be that we are working out karma accrued not in our last life but possibly some lives back in the chain of incarnations we have undergone.

We can be sure that as with all universal laws, the doctrine of karma is both fair and just. Its ultimate effect is evolutionary. We do not operate in a vacuum. It is crucial to understand that whenever we do, say or think anything it has consequences. And the results of those thoughts and deeds depend wholly on our intention at the time.

To give an example, it is widely recognised that suicide is the worst form of spiritual ineptitude with major long-term consequences. This is especially true if we kill ourselves to avoid the tests and trials of the lower self or to evade responsibilities for the effects of our actions. However, if someone deliberately sacrifices themselves in an act of altruism such as protecting others from harm, the motivation is entirely different.

The question often arises these days about the ethics of assisting those with incurable or debilitating illnesses to end their lives. This is an extremely difficult and delicate area for which there are no definitive answers. As brothers of humanity it should always be our duty to alleviate suffering wherever it is possible. And yet harsh as it may seem, an individual's suffering in whatever form is likely to be closely associated with the karma resulting from previous lives. It could be that as someone slips out of physical life, the final days of suffering contain the most important lesson that a person learns this time round on Earth School.

Some critics of this idea complain that the doctrine of karma inevitably produces a sense of fatalism, where people meekly accept their lot in this life and do nothing to improve it or themselves.

Our karma, however negative, can be the best teacher of all. Not only can we eventually learn to successfully deal with that karma we have accumulated previously, we can reduce its impact on future lives by our conduct now.

## Suffering

Virtually everyone experiences pain and suffering whether physically, mentally, emotionally or in some other way. Most people would avoid it if they could. And yet suffering is unavoidable. It is an integral part of our development. It is there to teach us important lessons and improve our conduct.

The main cause of our suffering is quite simple: it is ignorance of the spiritual and cosmic laws of life affecting us and everything else in the universe. This ignorance is fuelled by a purely materialistic view of the world and the illusions of reality created and reinforced by our physical senses.

## LIFE AFTER LIFE

We have all died and been re-born many times before. As the word reincarnation suggests, this does not happen just once but over and over again. You would think we might be getting used to it by now.

All over the world there is growing belief in the concept of reincarnation even among religions which teach otherwise. Although the idea of re-birth is firmly rooted in Hinduism and Buddhism, it is often significantly different to the Ageless Wisdom teachings.

Christianity and its sister religions of Islam and Judaism do not believe in the pre-existence of souls. They believe a 'use only once' soul is created for each new life and then sent off to an eternity in paradise or hell. Interestingly, until the 6th Century the Church embraced reincarnation as one of its central tenets. Then Christian politics intervened and it was outlawed.

Indeed, opinion surveys among the very many Christian sects around the world often show a surprisingly high proportion of believers firmly rooted to ideas of reincarnation. Catholics seem more persuaded of this than Protestants especially Methodists.

The Theosophical perspective is that there is no logic to the 'one life on Earth' point of view whatsoever. What can a human being learn in a single life especially if they die very young? Why would any self-respecting monad want to spend eternity in a paradise of some kind, however pleasant, when there is so much else to explore? It would be like being imprisoned in the world's most luxurious hotel – very agreeable for a while no doubt, but certainly not for eternity - however good the view and the room service.

If we accept that the purpose of all life is to evolve to ever greater perfection of consciousness then this evolution can only be achieved by hard work on the physical plane interspersed with periods of relaxation and assimilation in higher realms. It cannot be achieved by sipping metaphysical Martinis in Heaven's Hotel forever.

Groups of people within certain religions teach a variant of the re-birth idea. One idea known as transmigration or metempsychosis teaches that humans can re-incarnate in animal or plant form. But The Ageless Wisdom insists that once a human soul has individualised after passing through the lower kingdoms, it can never again return to them. It must remain part of the human project. It cannot return as an oak tree or a cat.

All progress comes through struggle. There was never a time when this was not the case. This is why the rough and tumble of the physical plane is so vital to our progress. The Earth is often referred to as a learning planet because it can be an extremely tough and challenging place to be on many levels. It is sometimes called Earth School.

So a succession of hundreds or even thousands of lives mediated by karma makes perfect sense in terms of the evolutionary grand plan. We will have had long lives and short ones, lives of pleasure and privilege as well as those scarred by poverty, disease, violence or squalor. We will have played many roles throughout this long series of incarnations and experienced many occupations, relationships, triumphs and tragedies. We will have been men and women, mothers and fathers, brothers and sisters, friends and enemies.

In Theosophy there has been much speculation about the sex we choose for each life. Do we alternate between men and women? This does happen but it appears to be more common for a reincarnating ego to spend a number of lives as a man or woman up to a maximum of around seven. Generally, it would appear that we choose the sex which best fits our intentions and purpose in any life.

It is often said that we incarnate with those who have been our friends, relatives or even associates in previous lives. Some speculate that although we are individualised souls we belong to collectives of souls with which we strongly identify.

The Ageless Wisdom describes evolution as cyclical. But imagine it also as a spiral progressively ascending to new levels. So in a particular life each one of us learns certain lessons (and undoubtedly fails to learn many others). The learning, abilities and knowledge we acquire and the experiences we gain are never lost. In fact they can be looked on as transferable skills. This means that in our next life we will emerge at the most elevated point we achieved in this one – and maybe slightly higher. Nothing can be lost.

It is generally recognised that young or child victims of conflict, natural catastrophe, pandemics or other causes may reincarnate quicker than those who have completed a full physical life-span. For example, the predominantly young troops who died in their millions in the World Wars I and II in the 20th Century may well have reincarnated rapidly in the immediately ensuing decades.

Knowledge of this doctrine of re-birth can hugely assist us here in our present lives. Why? Because it gives us a greater sense of responsibility and an urge to act wisely, creatively and compassionately. We know that if we fail to do this, there will be consequences somewhere down the line. If we appreciate that we are spiritual beings undergoing a human experience, we can derive far greater benefit from this life.

On the other hand, if we believe only in a solitary sojourn to this planet, it may entice us to act less responsibly. We are likely to be more eager to satisfy our lower, selfish desires, acting sometimes with cruelty and greed. 'Get what you can when you can' is often the attitude. But this is a blinkered and short-term view.

'I didn't believe in reincarnation in my past life, and I still don't.'

*Woody Allen*

*Above:* The 'untouchables' are the lowest of the Indian castes. Fighting against poverty and discrimination, they have chosen the name *dalit* (divided) to promote their cause.

What could be more exciting than to be a key player in an eternal continuum which elevates us to greater and greater heights, assuming that we put in the necessary struggle, sacrifice and effort? Heading off on an infinite adventure seems preferable to dwelling on the relatively niggling and trivial concerns of one life.

In religions which believe in re-birth of some kind, such as Hinduism, reincarnation has sometimes led to a passive fatalism. For example, some assert that it helps perpetuate India's pervasive and divisive caste system by arguing that those in lower social orders such as 'untouchables' are there because of their karma and should not be helped to improve their lot.

### Arguments against reincarnation

The chief argument is that it cannot be proved. In fact very few things can be proved beyond all doubt. Even the laws of physics undergo changes as new discoveries are made. And what would actually constitute proof? People's past life memories fail to convince the sceptics. There is no electronic equipment we can use to search for past lives. Perhaps we should invite the cynics to prove conclusively that reincarnation is a lie.

Another argument is that there is no physical evidence. This is not true. There are a large number of well-documented cases which offer strong evidence. Over the past few decades researchers have contacted thousands of people across the world who claim to recall previous lives. Many of them are young children who offer exhaustive and elaborate details of their immediate past lives. Often it turns out that these children died young – and presumably reincarnated quickly. When investigated complex details about people and places prove to be entirely accurate.

It is often asked why we cannot remember our past lives, although some people claim to be able to do so. Can you remember what you were doing three weeks last Tuesday or in mid-February thirty years ago? If we were burdened with all the memories of hundreds of previous lives we would be totally overwhelmed and unable to operate in our current one. And besides, given the often brutish nature of human history, our guilt about those whom we had maimed, killed, raped or exploited would probably drive us insane.

In the future when we have evolved further into the upper reaches of the human kingdom via experience and initiation, we will no longer see each life as separate like beads on a necklace. Instead, we shall see it as one continuous existence whether in physical bodies or furthering our self-development on the inner planes.

## THE MYTH OF DEATH

In the strict sense of the term there is no such thing as death. It is impossible to die in the way many people understand it. The death of the physical body leads merely to a change of consciousness – not oblivion. Death is a regular occurrence for us and we survive it because we return to physical life again and again. For a time we merely leave our physical bodies behind and spend time in non-material states assimilating and synthesising the experiences we have gained on Earth. We spend far longer out of the physical plane than we do on it.

Believing that we spend just a single life on this planet is not only absurd and illogical, it also promotes negative ideas of selfishness, greed and separation from each other, from nature and from the wider cosmos.

For a great many people death is their biggest fear and many would avoid it if they could. Often people do not like to talk about the subject regarding it as a morbid topic. Some hopelessly misguided people have themselves cryogenically frozen at death and housed in a cold-store until such time as medical science can find a way of resurrecting them and curing them of whatever disease caused their demise.

For materialists who accept no other reality than the physical, death can be a truly terrifying prospect. However, if you have a spiritual perspective and view death no more importantly than moving from room to room or changing clothes, then it simply becomes a doorway into another world. Knowing something about the process of dying, what happens and where you go gives you an enormous advantage over those who dread moving on fearing annihilation and oblivion.

Fear of death acts as one of the biggest impediments to a smooth transition into the post mortem world. It also creates lingering attachments to people and places especially in the immediate after-death state.

These days the vast majority of people do not die in their own homes but in the unfamiliar surroundings of hospitals or hospices. There are often invasive medical interventions up to the very end. And most disturbing for the dying person are the raw emotions of sadness and grief which friends and relatives display on their visits.

Silence and tranquility offer the best backdrop for those passing on. Powerful emotions create disruption and uncertainty for those about to depart. Medical staff in hospitals and hospices report that the dying person often waits for the nurse or relative to leave the room before passing on. This exit from life is for many an intensely private act.

'Sages do not grieve for the living nor for the dead. Never did I not exist, nor you, nor these rulers of men; nor will any one of us hereafter cease to be.'

*Bhagavadgita*

'As a man, casting off worn-out garments, taketh new ones, so the dweller in the body, casting off worn-out bodies, entereth into others that are new.'

*Bhagavadgita*

Our thoughts and state of mind at the moment we die are also of great importance. Not only do they affect our transition, but they may also have a bearing on our next life.

A lot of people – even those without any spiritual conviction – seem to intuitively adjust to death after first being angry, then in denial, then blaming someone before finally accepting their fate. With older people especially it is not uncommon to see them engaged in conversations with what we believe are imaginary beings. Perhaps some are already in contact with the astral world, which is the first port of call after death.

In the modern world the concept of a good death is rarely considered. And yet if we have had good lives why should its final climax necessarily be a negative thing? Why should we not have a good death? Death is only a negative concept for those who fail to understand what it really is.

It is a great opportunity and we should make the most of it.

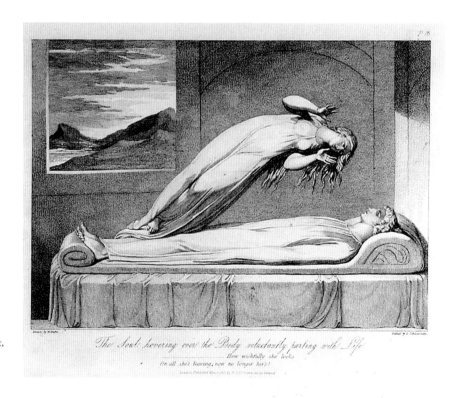

*The Soul hovering over the Body reluctantly parting with Life*

*Right:* A 19th Century illustration of Scottish poet, Robert Blair's poem *The Grave* (first published in 1743), depicting the soul leaving the body.

## THE AFTERLIFE STATES & WHAT HAPPENS WHEN WE DIE

The Ageless Wisdom teachings tell us that we spend far more time out of physical form than we do in human bodies – perhaps as little as seven per cent. These regular periods out of incarnation are an important part of our cyclic development. The period of death until the next rebirth is known by Tibetan Buddhists as the *bardo* state. Knowing something about what to expect can ease anxiety since fear is usually a product of ignorance.

Once we have breathed our last breath and all vital bodily functions cease, we begin the journey we have made many times before. Our energising principle (the etheric or energy/vital body) continues for some hours before itself ceasing. The Ageless Wisdom speaks of a silver cord linking our physical and astral bodies being finally severed.

At the moment of physical death human beings undergo a life review in which every single event and incident in their lives – however remote or forgotten - is re-run in a series of flash-backs. This takes only a few seconds. As the Higher Self (or Ego) re-lives every secret memory it detects the predominant patterns and ruling thoughts. These dictate exactly where on the next plane, the astral, the Ego will spend the bulk of its time.

As we shall see, we subsequently undergo not just one but a number of 'deaths'. Each is accompanied by a further life review in which we see all events unfold. There has been a lot of scientific study into death and many reports of people who have 'died' in accidents or during hospital operations but who have not made the final transition. These Near Death Experiences (NDEs) have been well documented and share many similarities.

People often describe travelling down a tube or tunnel and emerging into a world bathed in bright light where they are met by friends, relatives or sometimes strangers who communicate with them. Although individuals frequently wish to stay in this non-physical realm, they are told that it is not yet their 'time' and they must return to the physical plane to complete their 'mission'.

One surprising thing is that virtually everyone (even the spiritual sceptics) who has undergone an NDE comes back with a very different view of death and in virtually every case it no longer holds any fear for that individual.

There is much discussion as to how aware we are during this transitional process. Often it all takes place in a state of near unconsciousness or a dream-like state. Some, however, are able to perceive what happens.

## THE ASTRAL WORLD

We find ourselves on the astral plane, the world of desire and emotion – the place we retreat to each night during dream sleep. It is effectively a mirror image of the physical world. Everything on the physical plane has its astral counterpart.

In Theosophy the technical term for the dwelling place of astral entities is **kama-loka** (literally 'desire world' or 'shadow world'). Essentially, the astral or desire world is a place of purification (not dissimilar to the purgatory of the Christians) where we cleanse ourselves of the coarser aspects of ourselves before continuing our after-death journey.

When we do become aware of the astral world, what we find there is dictated almost exclusively by what we expect and by our prejudices or pre-conceptions. It is not an objective world, but a subjective one of our own creation. If we expect nothing to happen, probably nothing will - for a while at least.

Astonishingly, perhaps, sometimes people do not even initially realise that they have passed on. They notice very little difference because they are still rooted to familiar surroundings, possessions and people. Some are said to continue in this state for years. The realisation that something has changed comes when they can no longer feel physical objects or communicate with the 'living'.

Those holding literal or fundamental religious beliefs are likely to encounter what they believe. A Bible-thumping, hellfire and brimstone preacher, for example, might well encounter the very thing his fear has created – a snarling, horned devil pushing him menacingly towards the flames and sulphurous fumes. For him it is a self-fulfilling prophecy.

Overall, the astral world is a place of much greater freedom than in the physical realms. There are no longer the shackles, needs and limitations of the physical body. This means that there can be immense enjoyment and gratification. You can travel anywhere instantly. Opportunities for learning and new experience abound.

However, if your previous life involved purely physical pleasures there may be a degree of frustration since you no longer have a physical frame in which to indulge these passions. Those with an overly sex and drugs and rock 'n roll lifestyle or other strong addictive passions may find this environment particularly challenging.

There is much debate as to how long we remain in this transitory world and there are no definitive answers other than: the more spiritually evolved an individual, the less time spent in the astral world. This means that some could pass through in hours, days or months while others would languish here for years, decades or even centuries having more 'processing' work to do. One figure often quoted is that the

## The Akashic Records

Another key Theosophical principle is that of the Astral Light (known in Sanskrit as *akasa*). Pronounced 'akasha' it means 'brilliant' or 'luminous'. This is an all pervasive invisible force which produces a universal matrix or template for everything physical. It is a subtle, supersensuous essence which pervades all space and then differentiates into all forms of matter both visible and invisible

It can be regarded as similar in many ways to an electromagnetic field or like plasma. Victorian scientists referred to it as the aether.

Akasha is permanently impressed in everything on the physical, astral and mental planes. This indelible stamp leaves an eternal memory known as The Akashic Records, which can be accessed and read by those with the powers to do so. These records are effectively a unique and totally accurate record of everything that has ever happened.

Akasha is the fifth element or essence (quintessence) and is the aether of the Greek Stoics, an idea later resurrected briefly by 19th

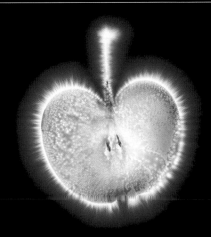

Century science and then abandoned. Akasha is not recognised at all by modern science – at least not yet. This could well be part of the missing link that science has strived so hard to discover for centuries.

The Astral Light reflects all the massed thoughts, ideas, actions and feelings of humanity – a whirlpool soup of mental, emotional and physical energy. This is the source of world consciousness.

Science has confirmed this in a number of ways. At great professional risk, the distinguished and very left

field biologist Rupert Sheldrake has conducted extensive work into what he terms morphogenetic or morphic fields. His extensive experiments add huge weight to the evidence that we know when someone is staring at us from behind.

Perhaps his most conclusive work involves elaborate experiments to prove that dogs know exactly when their owners are coming home. Sheldrake's experiments showed that even when normal routine patterns were broken the dogs stirred in anticipation, not only when their owners left work, but at the moment they intended to leave.

In the 20th Century the Russian scientist Semyon Kirlian photographed the energy fields of living creatures and plants which were seen as glowing auras. Significantly, the photographs showed the full pattern of a leaf even when a portion had been detached or a finger had been amputated. Developments from Kirlian's work are now used in medical diagnosis.

'average' person would typically spend the equivalent of a third of their Earth life in the world of desire – say 25 years for someone who lives into their seventies.

Those who die in childhood are likely to take new bodies relatively quickly. Those who die a sudden death in 'accidents', car crashes, crime or suicide will take longer to pass through the astral realms. If they die at the age of, say, 30 and would have otherwise lived to 80, they will have to spend the remaining 50 years before moving on to the next world. However, there are always exceptions.

Just as we re-lived all the events of our lives at the close of our last physical incarnation, at the end of our time in the astral realms we undergo what is often called the second death and a further life review. Unconsciously we move on. The astral bodies we have left gradually disintegrate.

We have purified ourselves as much as possible. Our three-fold Ego has assimilated the purest spiritual content of our lives. Now we spend time in the next realm, the mental world – providing we have accumulated enough mental material to assimilate there.

## Sub-planes of the Astral World

As with all the planes of existence, the astral world has seven distinct divisions or sub-planes. The lowest of these corresponds to the Christian hell or the eighth sphere of the Buddhists. Above that each plane is more refined and we gradually ascend to the level corresponding to our spiritual evolution and the degree to which we have mastered our emotions and desires.

The lowest or seventh sub-plane is a place sizzling with every variety of negativity – hate, revenge, violence and lust. It is described as the lowest slum of the afterlife and because of the Law of Attraction it draws in the very worst examples of humanity: mass murderers, recidivist criminals and those committing genocide, for example.

Above this, the sixth sub-plane is far less intimidating, sometimes compared closely to physical life

on Earth with its trivialities and minor concerns. Those here are said to find the place strangely discomforting. Many experience pain – on an emotional rather than physical level.

In the fifth and fourth sub-planes there is a distinct difference in atmosphere. This is a more pleasant place (except that it is more of a state of consciousness than an actual location). Here perceptions are heightened. Colours are often brighter and sounds sharper. The surroundings

are more etherealised with a radiant or luminous appearance.

The third sub-plane may be more familiar to people because it corresponds to the Hades of the Greeks, the Norse Valhalla, the Summerland of the Spiritualists or the happy hunting grounds of the indigenous tribes of North America. This is the natural habitat for those of unquestioning religious faith and literalist beliefs.

The second sub-plane is yet more refined, a place for the sensitive, artistic and intellectual. These creative types may work on their grand schemes, and concoct anything they like from fine buildings to entire landscapes.

Few seem to make it to what might be called the penthouse suite of the astral plane. This is apparently a refined place for the most selfless and those interested in acquiring spiritual knowledge.

## Astral inhabitants

The astral world is a landscape we often visit but which remains largely unfamiliar. Each one of us visits this realm every time we go to sleep. However, when we wake our recollections and perceptions of this plane are often garbled and confused. So at any point in time a third of the seven billion plus human beings in incarnation on Earth are in contact with the astral world.

And we are far from solitary voyagers in this world. It is a very busy and bustling place, teeming with life-forms – human, non-human and artificial.

Alongside those who sleep are those relatively small numbers of psychically developed people who have learned how to consciously access this zone of desire and emotion. And there is another very small category: advanced adepts who choose to remain here rather than moving on to the bliss of nirvana in the higher mental worlds.

Alongside the living there are the dead in various states of purification. As the lower self-based emotions are purged the astral body becomes what is known as a *shade*. When that is completely devitalised it becomes an astral *shell* which can sometimes be temporarily occupied by other entities such as nature spirits.

Finally, among the human dead are relatively rare remnants of long-gone developmental races of humanity. These are the vampires

*Above and background: The Garden of Earthly Delights* is the modern title given to a triptych painted by the Early Netherlandish master, Hieronymus Bosch. It dates from between 1490 and 1510, when Bosch was between about 40 and 60 years old, and is his best-known and most ambitious surviving work.

and werewolves of myth and legend – and staples of the movie industry.

Dwarfing the numbers of dead and living humans is an infinitely greater pool of non-human entities such as the elementals, nature spirits and devas. There are also a number of higher spirits residing here. The bodies of dead animals form a very large category, although having group souls they spend relatively little time in this world. Domesticated animals closer to having individualised souls will enjoy a longer stay.

It may surprise many to know that by far the biggest class of entities in the astral world are those which are created artificially both consciously and unconsciously. Every time we

think we create thought-forms because thoughts are living things. Those we create automatically and unconsciously are usually fairly transient. Their duration is in direct proportion to the power of the thought. This means that thought elementals created consciously – especially those created for magical ceremonies and occult rituals – can retain their powers for good or evil for decades, centuries or even millennia.

It is said that some of these astral forms created by the black magicians of Atlantis were so powerfully malignant that their effect is still felt negatively in the world today.

*Above:* Detail of *Constellation: Awakening at Dawn* (1941) by Spanish painter, sculptor and ceramicist, Joan Miró.

## THE MENTAL WORLD

The higher reaches of the astral world blend into the lowest of the next higher realm, the mental plane, sometimes known as the heaven world (Sanskrit **devachan**, 'land of the gods'). When we have completed the process of refining the astral body and assimilated its purest spiritual content into our permanent three-fold Ego, the astral body is cast aside.

This is where we undergo a second death and experience a further life review. We have now shed the last of our four transitory personality bodies. What remains is our permanent individuality – the three principles of higher mental, wisdom-intuition and spirit. These are effectively the enduring superstructure for the personality in each physical life.

In some cases people of limited mental development will spend only a short time on the mental plane or possibly bypass it altogether. There would be no point because there is little or nothing to process. On the other hand, some highly evolved people can spend a very long time indeed in this state of consciousness. The early Theosophists spoke of periods of 700, 1,200 or even 1,500 years between physical incarnations. There is much ongoing debate and speculation about this. Although numerically difficult to pin down, it appears that the more our higher spiritual principles are evolved, the longer we remain in this heaven world.

Just as the vibrations in the astral world are noticeably quicker than those in the physical, in the mental realms they are far quicker still. This is the place we go to experience the bliss or nirvana we have earned after our prolonged struggles through each individual incarnation. It is a place where we rest, recuperate and learn. Pain, distress, sorrow and evil are absent. Communication is instant since there are now no barriers between soul and soul. Language is unnecessary.

And we are free to create our own heaven world because after all, this is also a subjective place of the mind and the imagination. It depends on the energy and potency of our thoughts as well as our powers to visualise. It is effectively a blank canvas on which we can create. The mental world expands in direct proportion to our consciousness.

We have a unique overview here of our progress through physical bodies. We can potentially look back on the long meandering progression of past lives and identify the karmic causes which have shaped them. We can also sometimes get glimpses of the karma to be resolved in future lives. We may even get some insight into what those lives may involve.

Developed people come into the mental world fully conscious. Others may be far less aware of their environment.

As with all planes of existence there are seven sub-planes in the mental world. The lower four are said to have 'form' (Sanskrit, *rupa*). This substance is very rarefied compared to physical or astral material. The higher three planes are described as formless (*arupa*). Here the occupants have shed their lower minds of concrete thinking and operate only with higher thoughts.

A brief tour of these sub-planes gives us some idea of their workings. The lowest seventh plane is characterised by affection for family and friends, the sixth by religious devotion and the fifth by active work and philanthropy. The fourth-plane is described as speeding up the work of the Ego via the pursuit of spiritual, philosophical or scientific thought, service and artistic action.

On the formless sub-planes the third is the most populous and home to the 60-odd billion monads involved in human evolution. The second sub-plane offers opportunities for accelerated spiritual growth and offers access to influences from higher planes and more evolved entities.

Only relatively small numbers of masters and initiates enter the first sub-plane. Entry requirements include the achievement of integrated self-consciousness. All those gaining access to this level are fully aware that lower bodies are simply temporary vehicles of experience. Those on this plane see all their past lives as a single continuous life – whether in the body or out of it.

Although not perfection as such, this is a realm of ineffable beauty and as far removed from the Earth world as we can probably imagine,

But we cannot remain in this world of bliss forever. Sooner or later the impulse from our Higher Selves dictate that we must again resume life in bodies of flesh, blood and bone and reincarnate on Earth once again. Before we do there is the third of our life reviews in which we not only get a further review of our last life but – intriguingly an overview of the key events in the next life we have chosen from start to finish.

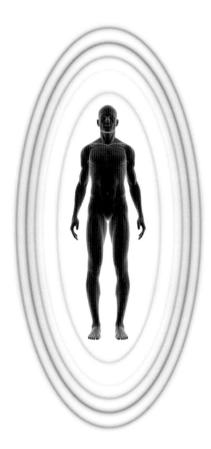

*Above:* The 'Auric Egg' is a term given to the invisible oviform envelope surrounding each of us, which contains and synthesises all the seven human principles from the spiritual to the physical. It is the repository of our monadic, spiritual, intellectual, mental, desire-based and vital energies. It is the source of the human aura. Essentially, it is eternal. Not only does it survive through the various cycles of reincarnation, but also through the greater cosmic cycles of manifestation and rest.

## RE-EMBODIMENT & RE-BIRTH

The mechanics of this are fairly complex and technical and so we shall attempt a simple explanation. During our time in the super-physical realms we have learned how to build a body which is suitable physically, mentally and astrally for our next incarnation.

Not only do we choose a time, place, culture, social position and other specific circumstances, but surprising as it may seem to some, we also choose our parents – those individuals most suited to providing our physical and hereditary make-up but not of course our soul qualities.

It is interesting to note that we incarnate over and over again with many of the same egos with whom we have previously associated. We will all play many different family roles as well as those of friends, family members, associates and even enemies. In each life the personalities are totally different and so are the relationships. In one life A is B's father. In another A and B are sisters. And in yet in another A and B are bitter rivals. This is often explained by the existence of 'soul groups', collectives of egos who share common bonds. This is not to be confused with the group souls of other kingdoms especially the animal.

Put basically, each of our bodies has what is known as a 'life-atom' or sometimes permanent atom which is retained when that body dissipates after death. These are actually evolving entities but can be regarded as mini-templates which will be re-used in the future. Formed into a sheaf, these permanent physical, vital, astral and lower mental life-atoms are introduced into the mother's womb not long after gestation. They are the basis of the new personality we shall assume for the next life.

This, as well as what happens to us, is also shaped by our accumulated karma from previous lives, some of which we shall need to deal with in this new incarnation. This karma is stored in what is termed an 'auric egg' – a sheath which surrounds us.

## THE FIVE SKANDHAS

As well as life-atoms and karma, there is another set of key influencing factors. These are the five *skandhas* or attributes which are always with us, including the after-death states. These can be regarded as attributes, traits or characteristics which are re-activated at birth. They are:

1. Form of the physical body
2. Bodily sensation
3. Perception and understanding of abstract ideas
4. Mental impressions
5. Consciousness and mental powers

There is another determining factor shaping our lives known as *dharma*, a Sanskrit word usually translated as duty but it also means a basic quality or characteristic. It is what moulds our understanding of spirituality, philosophy and science.

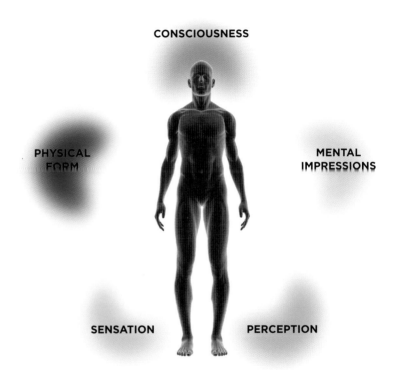

CONSCIOUSNESS

PHYSICAL FORM

MENTAL IMPRESSIONS

SENSATION

PERCEPTION

## The Dweller on the Threshold

This is a term coined by the eminent Victorian novelist Edward Bulwer Lytton in his novel *Zanoni*. Widely adopted by esoteric writers the term denotes the accumulated experience – much of it very negative – acquired through many incarnations. It is often remarked that when someone decides to accelerate their spiritual progress much of this 'grime' comes to the surface in often difficult and painful ways. Nevertheless, progress depends on our being able to deal with this challenging and unpleasant material and seek redemption and resolution through our own efforts.

The Dweller thrives on all our negativities and is fed and fuelled by our lower personality drives which are often very powerful. These drives are for such things as security, a desire for response and recognition from others as well as the constant itch for new experience. If these still dominate our lives – and for most of us they do – it means that The Dweller continues to lurk in the background hindering our psycho-spiritual development.

We all need to identify and determine the nature of our own dweller – and if we can, develop the appropriate counter-measures to de-activate and dismantle this malign presence. And yet merely recognising that there is such a poisonous entity haunting each of us is a helpful starting point. Before you fight a war you have to first know that you have an enemy – and who that enemy is.

As we progress through different lives we gradually become aware of this negative entity and we eventually begin to devise ways of neutralising it spiritually through humanitarian actions, service, sacrifice and altruism. When The Dweller has finally surrendered he is replaced by a much purer entity often called The Angel of the Presence. This represents a major victory.

## SOUL PURPOSE: MISSION OF THE HIGHER SELF

Each one of us coming into life has a particular purpose to achieve during those years in physical bodies. This is not set by some higher authority but by our own Ego or Higher Self. This consists of the permanent three parts of our makeup: higher mind, wisdom-intuition and spirit which are effectively our permanent souls.

Shaped by our cumulative karma – individually or collectively – we can regard our soul purpose as an objective we have to achieve or a mission we have to undertake in order to learn a particular lesson or lessons. It is a template for achieving some plan or aspiration in a given life. Naturally, we do not always succeed.

Often it takes us many years to discover what this purpose is – and then only vaguely. In some cases individuals never discover the real reason they chose a particular life. But when we do discover what this is, even if only vaguely, it can energise our lives with purpose and meaning.

If we steadfastly refuse to co-operate with our soul's intentions – or if we have no idea that such a reality exists – it is possible that our higher selves may terminate our present Earth adventure prematurely since the opportunity has been wasted.

## Glamour

We live in a glitzy and often amoral world oozing questionable values and hollow goals and which is largely ruled by the false gods of money and materialism. It is extremely difficult not to be attracted, seduced and addicted to the many supposed 'glamours' of life – especially those dictated by the sometimes overpowering desires of the lower self – wealth, power, status and recognition. These values are deeply ingrained in us, reinforced by social attitudes and especially by the media.

These many glamours have a hugely distorting effect on human beings' psycho-spiritual development because they encase us in the concrete of the immediate physical world and usually act as a barrier to higher states of consciousness.

Humanity has always had its heroes, heroines and role models. All cultures have recognised those influential individuals who have excelled in various endeavours. And yet the threadbare celebrity culture of today, which preoccupies so many people, has totally debased the idea of outstanding achievement – especially since most so-called celebrities have achieved little or nothing other than the inflation of their own egos. Those attaining real achievement do not seek the recognition lesser individuals crave.

However, it is not only materialistic people who fall victim to glamour. There is also spiritual glamour which can lead to arrogant and superior attitudes about our own progress, believing ourselves to be more advanced or refined than others.

'…the immediate problem before man and the significant contribution of the disciple is the dissipation of much of the glamour in which mankind is immersed and which, during the coming Aquarian Age, will largely disappear in connection with the astral life of the race. The point I would here make is to call attention to the fact that it is in meditation and in the technique of mind control that the thinkers of the world will begin to rid the world of illusion.'

Alice A. Bailey, *Glamour – A World Problem*

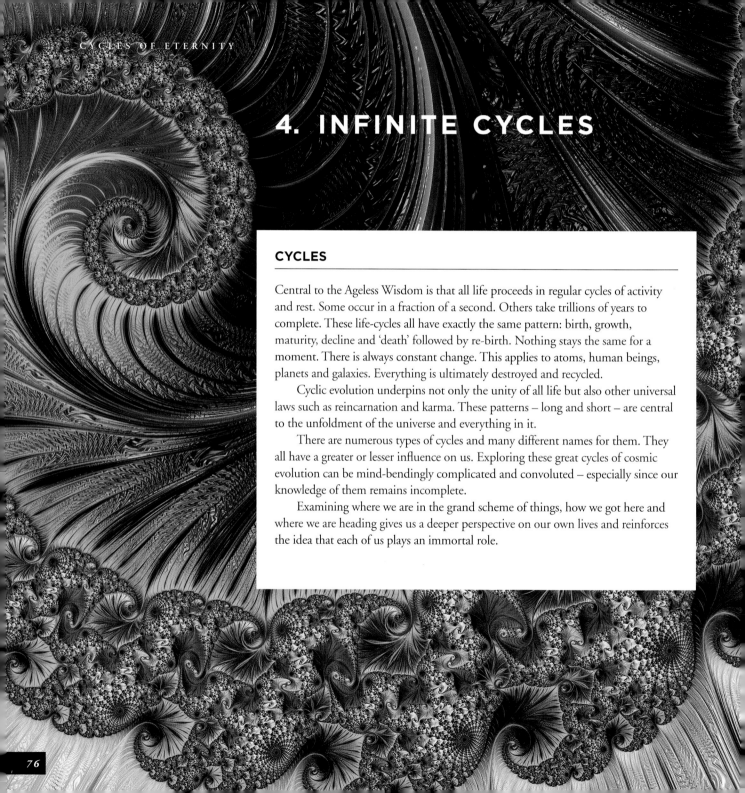

# 4. INFINITE CYCLES

## CYCLES

Central to the Ageless Wisdom is that all life proceeds in regular cycles of activity and rest. Some occur in a fraction of a second. Others take trillions of years to complete. These life-cycles all have exactly the same pattern: birth, growth, maturity, decline and 'death' followed by re-birth. Nothing stays the same for a moment. There is always constant change. This applies to atoms, human beings, planets and galaxies. Everything is ultimately destroyed and recycled.

Cyclic evolution underpins not only the unity of all life but also other universal laws such as reincarnation and karma. These patterns – long and short – are central to the unfoldment of the universe and everything in it.

There are numerous types of cycles and many different names for them. They all have a greater or lesser influence on us. Exploring these great cycles of cosmic evolution can be mind-bendingly complicated and convoluted – especially since our knowledge of them remains incomplete.

Examining where we are in the grand scheme of things, how we got here and where we are heading gives us a deeper perspective on our own lives and reinforces the idea that each of us plays an immortal role.

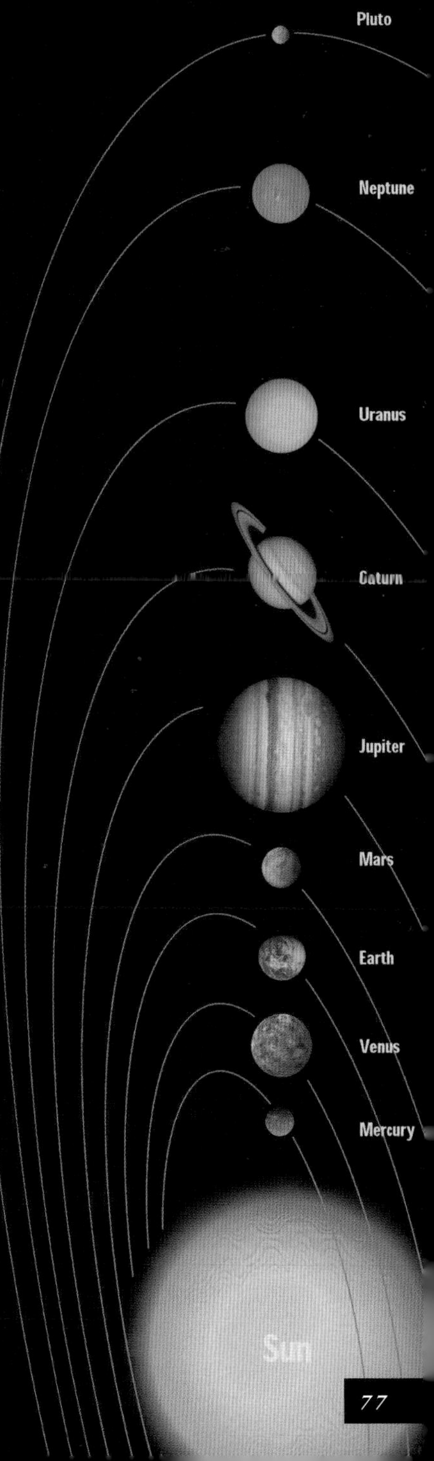

Pluto

Neptune

Uranus

Saturn

Jupiter

Mars

Earth

Venus

Mercury

Sun

## GLOBES

Because of its complexity, understanding the greater cosmic cycles of evolution is one of the areas which causes most difficulty and confusion for those interested in occult science.

The vast time-periods involved are almost beyond comprehension when our own individual lives are measured in a few decades.

Whether you look at it from the standpoint of conventional science or occult science, cosmic evolution is extremely mysterious and our understanding of it still remains very limited. So we shall confine our explanation to what we know about the development of our own tiny backyard of the universe – our own solar system.

Conventional science holds that our system consists of nine planets, although Pluto has recently been declassified and another even more distant planet on a vast elliptical orbit has been potentially identified. The Earth is identified as around four and a half billion years old. Although scientific knowledge of the solar system expanded exponentially during the 20th Century, we continue to encounter surprise discoveries.

The position of occult science is very different indeed since its explanation involves not just worlds of physical matter but those made of finer 'material' from other planes of existence. And occult science offers a more pervasive and organised explanation of the

### Evolution at a glance

| | |
|---|---|
| 7 Branch-races or nations | = 1 Sub-race |
| 7 Sub-races | = 1 Root Race |
| 7 Root races | = 1 Globe-period |
| 7 Globes | = 1 Chain |
| 1 Chain-period | = 7 Globes and 7 periods of activity |
| 1 Round | = 7 Globe-periods or; = 1/7th of a Chain-period |
| 7 Rounds | = 1 Chain-period |
| 7 Chain-periods | = A Scheme of Evolution (or 49 rounds and 343 globe-periods) |
| 7 (or 10) Schemes of Evolution | = the Solar System |

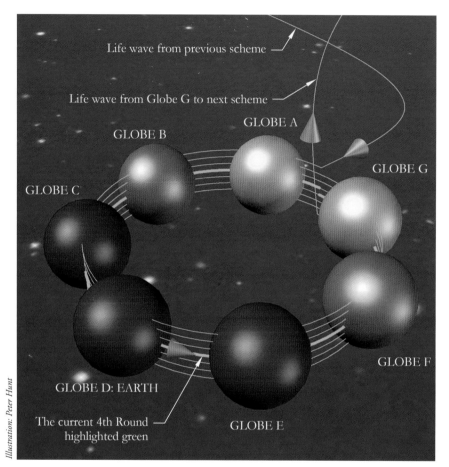

Life wave from previous scheme

Life wave from Globe G to next scheme

GLOBE A

GLOBE B

GLOBE G

GLOBE C

GLOBE F

GLOBE D: EARTH

GLOBE E

The current 4th Round highlighted green

*Illustration: Peter Hunt*

***Above:*** The Earth chain consists of three physical planets or globes – the Earth, Mars and Mercury. Globes A and G consist of lower mental matter while B and F are made of astral matter.

structure and working of our immediate cosmos than does conventional science.

The Ageless Wisdom asserts that the Earth is one of seven planets which are more commonly termed 'globes'. These seven globes form a 'chain'. The Earth chain is one of seven such chains which form our solar system.

In the Earth chain three of the globes including the Earth consist of physical matter. The others are Mars and Mercury. Two are formed from astral matter and a further two from lower mental matter. (Not all chains of globes are formed in this way.)

What this means is that a lower mental globe is one in which its most dense matter is lower mental. It has no astral or physical components. And an astral globe has no physical matter.

A single physical globe has counterparts of all the other states of matter from astral to spiritual. However, it does not occupy a separate or distinct space from these counterparts but the same space, although globes of higher matter are larger than those of lower matter. So we can regard a physical globe such as the Earth as not a single world but seven interpenetrating worlds. This is an unusually difficult concept to grasp.

The seven globes of a chain are normally referred to as Globes A, B, C, D, E, F and G. In the Earth chain Globes A and G are made of lower mental matter, B and F are formed by astral matter and C, D and E consist of physical matter. The Earth is designated Globe D while C is Mars and E is Mercury. The remaining globes have no names and are simply referred to by their letters. Each of these seven globes does have a unique location in space.

## ROUNDS & CHAINS

**Rounds:** The seven globes of a chain all exist simultaneously but only one is fully active and supporting various forms of life. The others remain in a dormant state. This happens sequentially. First Globe A becomes active and after a lengthy cycle this activity begins to wane before disappearing and being transferred to Globe B. Globe A then becomes inactive leaving just a 'nucleus' of life behind.

This process continues until activity on Globe B ceases and is passed on to Globe C. When this cycle is over activity moves on to Globe D (our present physical Earth globe).

The period during which the life-wave is active on a globe is known as a ***globe-period*** or ***world-period***. The passage of the life-wave around all seven globes is called a ***round***. The life-waves, three on the involutionary arc of descent and four on the evolutionary, are sometimes called 'agents of the law'.

When a round has been completed from Globes A to G the entire cycle begins again on Globe A until a second round is completed on Globe G. This continues until all seven rounds have been completed on all seven globes.

So we can see that a round consists of seven globe- or world-periods and that an entire cycle of seven rounds (known as a chain-period) is made up of 49 globe-periods. This is, of course, a radically different explanation from that conventionally offered by contemporary science.

**Chains:** Including the Earth chain there are seven\* such chains in our system. When a chain-period is completed its globes disintegrate and are then re-constituted to make seven new globes. These seven pass through seven rounds of activity and are then broken up to form seven new globes. This process occurs seven times through the seven chains (each of seven globes). This is a very clear illustration of how the number seven plays such a crucial role in occult science.

As we have seen, each globe consists of different types of matter from the coarsest physical to the finest spiritual matter. For example, the first and seventh chains have globes of only spiritual (atmic) matter, the second and sixth consist entirely of wisdom-intuition (buddhic). Only the third, fourth and fifth have physical globes.

During the disintegration of globes there is a period of rest and assimilation before

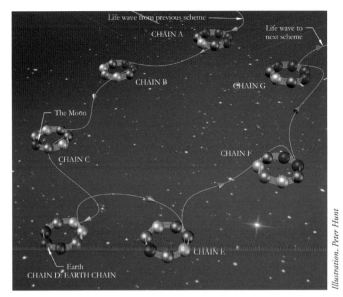

*Illustration. Peter Hunt*

**Above:** How the Earth chain fits into the seven-fold chain of globes which make up the solar system.

\* To complicate matters further, there are also schools of thought which identify ten and sometimes twelve planetary chains.

further activity resumes. This cycle, like all others, is a clear illustration of the Law of Rhythm.

In each chain a kingdom of nature moves up a step. For example, the previous chain to the current Earth Chain was the Moon Chain. At that stage in our development we were Moon Chain members of the animal kingdom. After progressing to the Earth Chain we permanently gravitated into the animal kingdom.

So where are we at the moment in the grand scheme of things? We are in the fourth chain of our Scheme of Evolution – at the very lowest level of materiality throughout the entire process. We have completed the involutionary process and are preparing for evolutionary ascent. We are in the fourth round of our own planet, Globe D.

An entire series of seven chains make up a Scheme of Evolution and seven (or ten) of these make up the solar system. As we can see this takes an almost incalculable period of time. However, the human evolutionary project will play a central role in this grand unfoldment.

Since this this is such a vast and complex subject only the most essential core details have been outlined. Nevertheless it is fascinating to see just how far our own kingdom of nature – the human – has progressed and indeed how far it has yet to travel.

If nothing else, this explanation gives us some kind of perspective of the eternal journey in which we are all engaged. And it should boldly demonstrate how our current life might be compared to a comma in a very large book.

## Yugas and Kalpas

Not much precise information is available about the durations of chains, rounds and globe-periods but ancient texts, originating in India and often quoted, identify precisely how long each age lasts. The word often used for age is *yuga*. There are four separate ages:

| | |
|---|---|
| Krita Yuga (The Golden Age) | 1,728,000 years |
| Treta Yuga (The Silver Age) | 1,296,000 years |
| Dvapara Yuga (The Bronze Age) | 864,000 years |
| Kali Yuga (The Iron or Dark Age) | 432,000 years |
| Total (a Maha Yuga or Great Age) | 4,320,000 years |
| 71 Great Ages or 1 Manu | 306,720,000 years |

We can see there is a mathematical relationship between these ages. Our current age, the Kali Yuga (which began about 5,000 years ago) is half the length of the previous age, a third the length of The Silver Age and a quarter the length of The Golden Age. In the ancient tradition this is extended further:

| | |
|---|---|
| 14 Manus | 4,294,080,000 years |
| Intervals between Manus (Equivalent to 6 Great Ages) | 25,920,000 years |
| 14 Manus = 1,000 Great Ages = 1 Day of Brahma | 4,320,000,000 years |
| plus 1 Night of Brahma | 4,320,000,000 years |
| 360 Days and Nights of Brahma = 1 Year of Brahma (*kalpa*) | 3,110,400,000,000 years |
| 100 years = Age of Brahma | 3,110,400,000,000 years |

## PRECESSION OF THE EQUINOXES

Perhaps one of the most important cycles – and one of the most widely recognised – is the zodiacal cycle of 25,920 years, known as the precession of the equinoxes or The Great Sidereal Year. It consists of twelve sub-cycles of 2,160 years, each representing a sign of the zodiac. These sub-cycles mirror the unfoldment of planetary consciousness. Each of these 'signs' colours the age in which it predominates.

For example, we are currently moving out of the Age of Pisces which began around the time of Christ and this has overshadowed and shaped both world events and human psycho-spiritual development. It is characterised by devotion and this has been mirrored in the fanatical allegiance towards religious, political and even scientific ideas. Prior to this and extending back to around 2,500 BCE was The Age of Aries which influenced the religions of the Middle East especially Judaism. Prior to that was the Age of Taurus which spawned – among other things – the mithraic or bull-worshipping religion of Crete.

For some time – some say as far back as the 17th Century – we have been moving out of the Age of Pisces and into the new Age of Aquarius about which so much is written, especially in terms of it being a new golden age. This age has a very different character to its predecessor. Devotion will give way to more creative and synthetic thinking. The urge to compete may well be overshadowed by the need to co-operate.

It is important to understand that there is a long changeover period between these ages. One does not suddenly end and the other immediately begin. Over many centuries the influence of a particular age weakens as its successor strengthens.

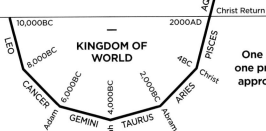

**SINE WAVE DIAGRAM OF LONG TERM HISTORY**

One complete cycle equals one precession of equinoxes - approximately 25,920 years.

### Astrology

This is one of the longest-established esoteric sciences with origins across the globe. The Chaldeans, Babylonians, Hebrews, Greeks and Romans all had their zodiac-based systems. The Hindus and Chinese also had their systems. Interestingly, despite geographical and historical gulfs, nearly all of these feature twelve signs.

Today there remain a number of different systems, each with their own variations. For example, vedic astrology bears little resemblance to contemporary Western astrology; and esoteric astrology represents another radically different interpretation.

## Seven Ages of Man

**0 - 7 years**
The child grows physically and achieves self-consciousness.

**7 - 18 years**
The soul has fully entered the body and this time is spent in education and preparation for adult life.

**19 - 30 years**
This is the stage where the young adult begins to make their way in the world, establishing relationships, starting families and careers.

**30 - 40 years**
This marks the mid-point of our life as adults and we begin to mature in mind and body.

**40 - 50 years**
By this age our priorities are changing and this is often the time when people begin to ask the big questions in life and feel the need to begin exploring their own spirituality.

**50 - 65 years**
By this age some of our energy will be depleted, although we may remain active physically and mentally. This is where the spiritual urge really kicks in for some people.

**65 years onwards**
In this final stage we have hopefully reached a sense of equilibrium and inner balance, as well as a mature and rounded view of the world. We are no doubt showing signs of having spent six and a half gruelling decades in physical bodies. But internally, this can be the most productive part of our lives as we now have time to devote to our inner life without the previous time constraints of career or family.

*Left: The Seven Ages of Man*, 1980, by Richard Kindersley. A cast aluminium totem pole sited in the courtyard at Baynard House, Queen Victoria Street, London.

## PERSONAL CYCLES

We are all part of vast cosmic cycles but each one of us also has a series of personal rhythms. These consist not only of our ray structure, karma and soul purpose but wider astrological and other planetary cycles such as the phases of the moon. They affect us at every level of our being.

We all respond to these things very differently. There are 'larks' who rise at dawn and enjoy the sunrise while there are 'owls' who are more comfortable late at night. We all have 'off days' when we are de-energised, depressed or despondent. We also have those days when everything locks into place and life is agreeable and harmonious.

While we cannot begin to understand the precise workings of these cycles, knowing they exist can be of great help to us as we attempt to gain a greater understanding of ourselves. The Law of Rhythm specifies that nothing stays the same for ever – even our good or bad moods. Knowing that we are subject to cycles can assist us in creating a firmer inner balance.

# 5. A BOUNDLESS UNIVERSE

## NO BEGINNING, NO END

The universe is eternal with neither beginning nor end but undergoing a cyclic period of manifestation and activity followed by a period of obscuration and rest. Infinity and eternity are difficult ideas to absorb – because of our limited perception and finite minds.

The Universal Mind appears as the entire infinite cosmos around and beyond us. Although a unity, it energises as a trinity. This idea appears in a number of different religions. In Christianity this overall consciousness or Cosmic Logos is expressed as God the Father, God the Son and God the Holy Ghost. In Hinduism it appears as Brahma the creator, Vishnu the preserver and Shiva the destroyer. In the Egyptian pantheon they appear as Osiris, Horus and Isis. Matter, life and consciousness are the three aspects of this unity. Closely linked with the work of the Cosmic Logos are the seven Cosmic Planetary Logoi. Every star in the universe involved in the evolution of life belongs to one of these seven.

The overarching entity in charge of our solar system is known as the Solar Logos. We are all parts of this vast entity. As mentioned earlier, like the Universal Mind or Cosmic Logos itself, the Solar Logos also operates as a trinity. In the Ageless Wisdom and Theosophical teachings this is usually referred to as the First Logos representing will or divinity-humanity (father), Second Logos representing wisdom or life-form (son) and Third Logos representing activity or force-matter (holy ghost).

The creation of the universe involves what are usually called three 'outpourings' of force but they do not occur in the order you may expect. These are forces of unimaginably stupendous power. If they reached us in an unmodified state they would destroy us.

The first outpouring comes from the Third Logos of activity and descends through all the planes to the densest form of physical matter. This force creates the seven planes of being. The cosmos solidifies and galaxies, stars, solar systems and planets are created along with the basic elements of earth, fire, air, water and aether. This process is known as involution.

The second outpouring comes from the Second Logos, which also descends as far as the lowest form of physical matter but then ascends to the lower mental plane.

The third outpouring originates from the First Logos, that of will. This energises the higher levels of existence down as far as the higher mental plane.

These three outpourings set the template for the newly created universe but because of their potency they have to be stepped down into seven lesser forces. These energy streams are known as the seven rays.

## The Three Outpourings

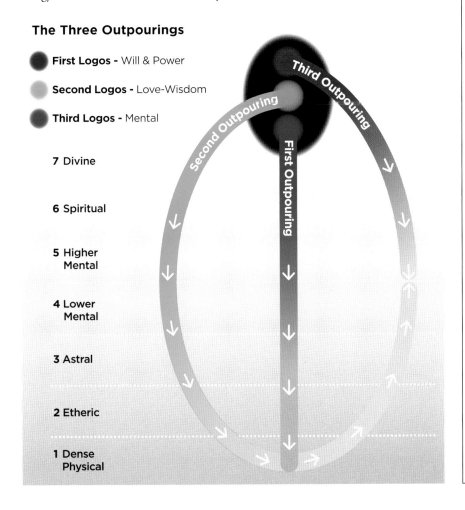

**First Logos -** Will & Power

**Second Logos -** Love-Wisdom

**Third Logos -** Mental

7 Divine

6 Spiritual

5 Higher Mental

4 Lower Mental

3 Astral

2 Etheric

1 Dense Physical

Third Outpouring

Second Outpouring

First Outpouring

## A triple force

All matter is permeated by three qualities or characteristics but these are intimately blended together rather than separated. These are known as the three *Gunas*:

*Sattwa* (creation): This is the quality of goodness, truth, reality and purity.

*Rajas* (preservation): This represents passion, longing or activity – nature's elemental urge to constantly change.

*Tamas* (destruction): This stands for darkness, ignorance and illusion as well as inertia and rest.

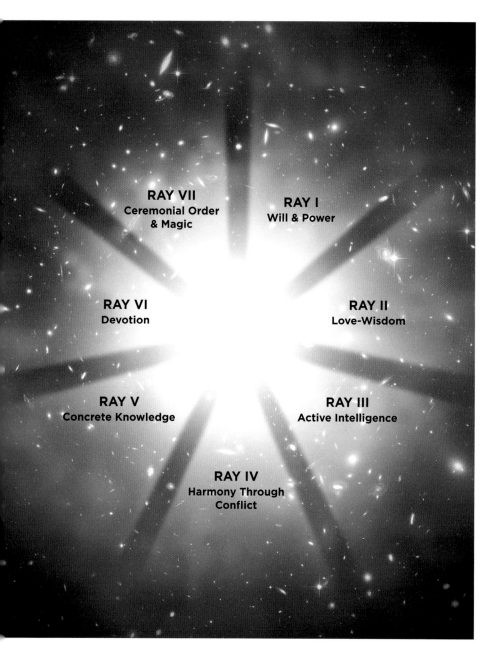

RAY VII
Ceremonial Order
& Magic

RAY I
Will & Power

RAY VI
Devotion

RAY II
Love-Wisdom

RAY V
Concrete Knowledge

RAY III
Active Intelligence

RAY IV
Harmony Through
Conflict

## THE SEVEN RAYS

Put simply, these are seven distinct cosmic forces, each with a unique flavour which colours the lives of individuals and shapes the world and the solar system.

Each person's monad or spirit remains permanently on one of the first three major rays of aspect. Of the 63 billion monads involved in current human evolution, three billion are on Ray I with 30 billion each on Rays II and III.

The soul or Ego can be on any ray for many incarnations but switches to one of the first three when it reaches an advanced stage of spiritual development. Most are on Rays II and VI with very few on Ray I and even fewer on Ray IV. As we move into a new cycle more people will have VII soul rays.

Overall our four-fold personality is on one ray while its physical, astral and mental bodies also each respond to specific rays. The combinations of these rays (along with our individual and collective karma) influence our lives to a far greater extent than most people realise.

It is customary to use Roman numerals to represent the seven rays.

## CHARACTERISTICS OF THE RAYS

### I: Will & Power

The first ray corresponds to the first aspect of the trinity, the creator (in Christianity, God the Father) and its characteristics are power, strength, determination, leadership, courage, self-reliance and independence. It is the ray of the leader, soldier or explorer. This ray plays a crucial role in the evolution of form. It therefore rules the human physical body. *Negative qualities:* hunger for power, selfishness, pride and rigidity.

### II: Love-Wisdom

The second ray represents the second aspect, the preserver (God the Son) and its qualities are spiritual sympathy, compassion, intuition, insight and generosity. It produces the healer, the humanitarian and the teacher. It represents impersonal, universal love based on the unity of life. It assists in the building of new forms to replace old ones. *Negative qualities:* impracticability, over sentimentality and lack of discrimination in helping others.

### III: Active Intelligence

The third ray is the third aspect, (the Holy Ghost) and exhibits the power of transformation and regeneration. Its features are creative imagination, deep understanding, analytical skills, assimilation of ideas and the application of knowledge as well as dignity, tact and impartiality. This ray produces scholars, diplomats, business directors, bankers and judges. *Negative qualities:* aloofness, coldness, cruelty, failure to give support as well as a tendency to be deceitful or unscrupulous.

### IV: Harmony Through Conflict

The characteristics of the fourth ray involve concepts of stability, beauty, harmony, balance, creativity and rhythm. Those with this ray also show a strong sense of equilibrium, symmetry, form and an aesthetic appreciation of all that is beautiful in life, nature and the arts. This is the ray of the artist, interpreter or mediator. It is the ray which humanity finds itself on at this time. *Negative qualities:* self-indulgence, extravagance, recklessness, conceit and dramatic mood swings.

## Rays shape countries

The destiny of every nation is shaped and governed by both a soul ray and a personality ray. Among the leading countries of the world only the United Kingdom, USA, Canada, Australia and Norway have the second ray of love-wisdom on the soul level.

Their personality rays vary: UK (I), USA (VI), Canada (I), Australia (VII) and Norway (IV).

Africa as a continent has a sixth ray soul and a seventh ray personality while India has a first ray soul and a fourth ray personality. Russia has a seventh ray soul and sixth ray personality.

No country has a soul and personality on the same ray.

## V: Concrete Knowledge

The fifth ray is concerned with the inquiring, analytical and deductive mind along with the acquisition and dissemination of knowledge. It concerns analytical skills, logic, patience, thoroughness of inquiry and detailed examination of facts. Truth, mental detachment and accuracy are its keynotes. It produces scientists, mathematicians and lawyers. *Negative qualities:* self-centredness, materialism, a sense of separation, pride, meanness and being too critical or pedantic.

## VI: Devotion

This sixth ray encompasses ideas of total commitment and even self-sacrifice to a cause or idea especially in terms of religion and politics. It is about fiery enthusiasm, loyalty, one-pointedness, adoration and even martyrdom as well as sympathy for others' suffering. Those in this ray are mystics, religious devotees, saints and evangelists. *Negative qualities:* blind devotion to personalities, intolerance, fanaticism, impulsiveness and being overly emotional.

## VII: Ceremonial Order & Magic

The seventh ray is centred on organised activity, precision, grace, skill and nobility of conduct and character. Its hallmarks are ceremony, discovery, dignity, pageantry, attention to detail and magic. One key feature is the discovery of and co-operation with nature's hidden forces. Those on this ray are those concerned with ceremony and ritual, arts producers, priests or magicians. *Negative qualities:* love of power and office, bureaucracy, playing politics, regimentation and using people as pawns.

These rays have particular influences during different periods of history. For example, The Age of Pisces is making way for the Age of Aquarius. The Piscean Age was governed by Ray VI whereas the Aquarian Age is ruled by Ray VII. This means that the values of the new age will be very different from the preceding one. Devotion to existing structures – religious, financial, political, scientific – will gradually give way to new forms of organisation based not so much on individuality, greed and competition but on group working, sharing and co-operation.

Times of major transition such as this are always accompanied by turmoil and upheaval. It is abundantly clear today how this change of ray is causing such global convulsions especially in the sphere of politicised religion.

*Note:* There are a number of variants in the names for these rays.

## FORCES & ENERGIES

There are a number of fundamental forces and exotic energies mentioned throughout the Ageless Wisdom – none of them as yet recognised by mainstream science. These forces impact on us and everything else in a myriad of mysterious ways, although we are aware of some of their effects. At present, science recognises only four forces:

1. Gravity
2. Electromagnetic energy
3. Strong nuclear force.
4. Weak nuclear force

The conventional scientific view currently is that gravity is the driving force in the universe. However, there is an emerging view that we may well inhabit an electric universe instead.

Drawing on aeons of esoteric research, occult science has identified a number of other energies:

### Prana

This means vitality and is sometimes also known as ch'i (from the Chinese). It is a universal and pervasive energising life principle permeating every being and object. It is the expression of force of the second logos (love-wisdom) and is transmitted and stepped down by the devas. It is often represented as breath. There are different types of prana operating at solar and planetary level as well as in the lower kingdoms.

Prana awakens desire within us and is infused into our physical bodies via the astral. When we die most of this energy returns to its source, although that suffused with our own life-atoms is retained for future use.

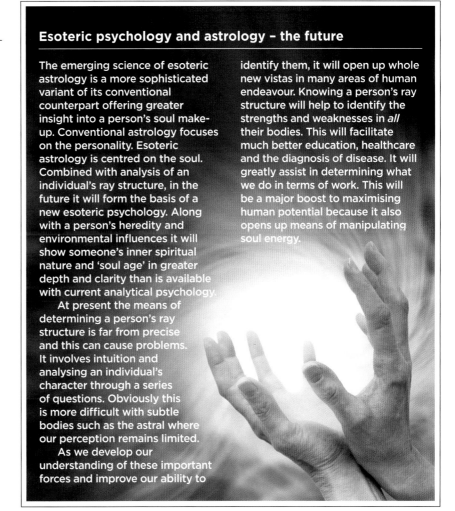

## Esoteric psychology and astrology – the future

The emerging science of esoteric astrology is a more sophisticated variant of its conventional counterpart offering greater insight into a person's soul make-up. Conventional astrology focuses on the personality. Esoteric astrology is centred on the soul. Combined with analysis of an individual's ray structure, in the future it will form the basis of a new esoteric psychology. Along with a person's heredity and environmental influences it will show someone's inner spiritual nature and 'soul age' in greater depth and clarity than is available with current analytical psychology.

At present the means of determining a person's ray structure is far from precise and this can cause problems. It involves intuition and analysing an individual's character through a series of questions. Obviously this is more difficult with subtle bodies such as the astral where our perception remains limited.

As we develop our understanding of these important forces and improve our ability to identify them, it will open up whole new vistas in many areas of human endeavour. Knowing a person's ray structure will help to identify the strengths and weaknesses in *all* their bodies. This will facilitate much better education, healthcare and the diagnosis of disease. It will greatly assist in determining what we do in terms of work. This will be a major boost to maximising human potential because it also opens up means of manipulating soul energy.

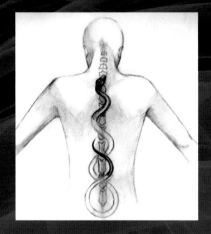

### Kundalini

This hugely potent and potentially destructive energy is often called the 'serpent fire' in Eastern traditions. It is portrayed as a coiled serpent in the lowest chakra at the base of the spine.

It manifests as the third aspect of the logos during the first outpouring of force. It originates deep within the fiery centre of the Earth. Having completed its involution it is now on the path of return and works through the bodies of living things. It burns away the 'dross' as it works its way to open our seven chakras via the sushumna.

If this energy is forced, for example through extreme forms of yoga or other practises, it can be especially dangerous to the brain and can even prove fatal. Chakras open in attunement with individual spiritual development.

### Fohat

This is a Tibetan term used to describe another fundamental force mentioned extensively in Theosophical writings. Fohat is the guiding super-force of nature and the power behind all manifestation. It means 'primordial light' or cosmic electricity and it animates every atom. It is the 'bridge' in which ideas from the Universal Mind are impressed on the substance and fabric of the universe via the laws of nature. HPB described fohat as "personified electric vital power", adding, "he is the steed and thought the rider."

There are as many types of this guiding intelligence as there are worlds. It is constantly active from the beginning to the end of a universe or solar system, building and destroying forms and so ensuring perpetual change.

# 6. OTHER AVENUES OF AWARENESS

## ALCHEMY: THE ANCIENT SCIENCE OF TRANSMUTATION

Alchemy is popularly seen as bearded sorcerers slaving over hot ovens pursuing the forlorn hope of turning base metals like lead into gold by creating the Philosopher's Stone. Sometimes it involved the production of an Elixir of Life which would offer longevity or spiritual illumination.

Although alchemy probably originated from metal technology it has little to do with producing gold ingots. Its roots go back to Egypt, China and India. Alchemy is essentially the science of spiritual transmutation in which participants refine and purify the lower parts of their nature into something more lofty and evolved.

Science has shown that it is possible to convert one element into another. This was first shown by the scientist Ernest Rutherford in 1919 when he used alpha radiation to turn nitrogen into oxygen via a nuclear reaction.

A few practical alchemists remain in business but few, if any, expect to get rich.

*Right: The First Stage of the Great Work,* better-known as the *Alchemist's Laboratory.* The drawing of the laboratory is credited to architectural painter Hans Vredeman de Vries (1527–1604) and shows Khunrath in his laboratory.

*Above:* A votive plaque known as the Ninnion Tablet depicting elements of the Eleusinian Mysteries, discovered in the sanctuary at Eleusis (mid-4th Century BC).

*Right:* Remains of the Sanctuary of the Great Gods at Samothrace, where mysterious rites took place which were open to both slaves and free people.

## MYSTERY SCHOOLS

Sometimes referred to as The Mysteries, these were ancient seats of knowledge established by advanced members of humanity to teach morality, reduce cruelty and provide a spiritual uplift. They were also closely concerned with teaching the secrets of death.

Many ancient civilizations such as Chaldea, Babylon and Egypt had their mystery schools but they are more popularly associated with Greece and later with the Roman empire. The mysteries were strictly divided into two distinct sections – the Greater Mysteries and the Lesser. The Greater consisted of study and initiation for those deemed suitable for advanced teaching while the Lesser were composed of dramatic rites and ceremonies for the masses. The Greater Mysteries were jealously guarded and stories abound of the uninitiated straying into their buildings and sometimes paying for their curiosity with their lives.

The Greek mystery schools at Eleusis and Samothrace taught the Greater Mysteries and this included explanations of the myths of the old religions.

## SYMBOLS

Symbols are central to the study of esoteric ideas. They have a primal power enabling them to convey more than words ever can. They survive down the generations, concealed and then resurrected. With ancient and esoteric origins they often work on the sub-conscious level and have a deep resonance.

Symbols are extremely potent and this is why they feature so widely in the modern world from emblems on flags and in commercial branding to religious symbols and everyday design. An American dollar bill is full of esoteric symbolism such as the all-seeing eye in the pyramid.

Many symbols are common to disparate cultures at different times in history – for example, the circle, which represents the Earth. Various forms of the swastika have been used over many thousands of years. One of humanity's oldest glyphs, it symbolises the continuity of the wheel of eternal life. But following its ubiquitous use by the Nazis it is now a degraded symbol of hate, violence and oppression. However, Hindus still use it, widely maintaining its original meaning as one of the ways of representing the continuity of existence.

The emblem of the Theosophical Society consists of seven different symbols. At the top is the Sanskrit script for *om*, the sacred word of Hindus and Buddhists in India. Although difficult to translate it represents the divine harmony of the universe. It also represents the three-in-one logos. Below this is the whirling cross or swastika (now used in a softened and modified form). This represents the process of becoming. Connected to the cross is the snake swallowing its own tail known by the Greek Gnostics as the *ouroboros*. It represents the boundary of the universe. The two interlaced triangles forming a six-pointed star, sometimes called The Seal of Solomon, reflect the idea that spirit and matter are interdependent. The dark downward-pointing triangle symbolises matter and the light upward-pointing triangle represents spirit or consciousness. At the centre of the six-pointed star is the *ankh*, the ancient Egyptian symbol for life itself. The six points of the cross and the ankh represent the seven principles of the universe. All these symbols signify the same thing – the unity of the cosmos and the correspondences which exist throughout the universe. The motto reflects the idea that reality is greater than the sum of its parts and that it is beyond human conception.

Symbols (and myths) have been used widely to hide deep truths from the uninitiated. For example, the alchemists who thrived across Europe in the Middle Ages made extensive use of symbols to disguise a potentially powerful knowledge from the

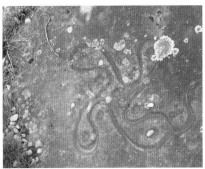

*Top:* The seal of the Theosophical Society.

*Above:* The Swastika Stone, located on Woodhouse Crag on the northern edge of Ilkley Moor in West Yorkshire. The design is unique in the British Isles, but its close similarity to Camunian rose designs in Italy have led some to theorise that the two are connected. Troops stationed in Ilkley during the Roman occupation were recruited from the Celtic Lingones, a tribe native to Gaul, but in around 400 BC, some migrated across the Alps to the Adriatic coast. Some believe the Ilkley Lingones were recruited from here rather than from Gaul. It is possible that the Italian Lingones passed through the Valcamonica region at some point, took on the swastika designs they found as part of their tribal symbolism, and carved it on the nearby moor when stationed in Ilkley.

profane, who would misuse these ideas. Alchemical literature is full of a baffling array of imagery featuring birds, hermaphrodites, lions, kings and mythical creatures which represent different aspects of the science of transmutation. These symbols disguise far more than they convey of details of their Magnum Opus (Great Work) – and deliberately so. And there was often no common agreement as to what these symbols represented.

*Clockwise from top:* the US dollar bill is replete with occult symbolism, especially the all-seeing eye in the pyramid; the pentagram, a five-pointed star enclosed in a circle, represents spirit triumphing over matter, but when inverted means the opposite, and is often used to represent satanic intent; in Chinese philosophy the interaction of yin (negative, dark and feminine) with yang (positive, bright and masculine) influences all living things; The Eye of Horus, an ancient Egyptian glyph signified royal power, good health and protection.

## RELIGIONS

Religions have guided mankind down the ages and their influence remains central in many people's lives – and their sole spiritual outlet. They have no doubt played their part not only in rescuing our ancestors from barbarity but also in promoting rudimentary spiritual awareness, creating basic morality and helping the development of civilizations. But these faiths have also produced tyranny, mass manipulation and the deaths of millions of people.

They continue to play a pivotal role in our world, although many are in conflict with each other or antagonistic to opposing factions within the same faith. In parts of the West in particular increasing numbers of people are either angered by religion or feel it is entirely irrelevant to their lives. Some feel that spirituality should no longer be the preserve of religious organisations and their mediators. More and more people describe themselves as spiritual but not religious. They want a spiritual life without the dead-letter dogma, blind faith and overblown ritual that some religions still peddle.

A number of distinguished occult writers have argued that religion causes the vast bulk of the world's problems. As this book is being written, large sections of the Islamic world especially is convulsed by warring rival branches and fundamentalist factions intent on destroying all other world views.

It is true to say that religions have always been highly political. Traditionally and even today religions are guilty of hijacking and monopolising spirituality with the clear message that God can only be accessed through them and their representatives such as priests. This is why they are seen by some as an increasingly inappropriate vehicle for spiritual development.

It is also interesting to note how every mainstream religion has downgraded the role of women and excluded them from its hierarchy. In a move that took decades to achieve, the Anglican Church now allows both women priests and bishops.

Throughout history mankind has concocted a wide variety of religions which broadly form into two distinct groups: those believing in a single God (monotheistic) or in a number of deities (polytheistic). Christianity, Islam and Judaism believe in a single God but also promote the idea of lesser spirits such as angels. Hinduism believes in a single God – Brahma – assisted by many millions of lesser spirits.

It is therefore not a contradiction to imagine an overall intelligence – the Universal Mind – guiding countless hierarchies, which are part of itself.

## Numbers

This has always been an important area of occult work and the cycles of eternity operate on strictly mathematical lines. Numbers are woven into nature – seen in the spiral structures of nautilus shells or galaxies and in countless other ways.

Numbers have great significance and power. Understanding how they developed and what they mean offers great insight into the inner workings of ourselves, our immediate world and the wider cosmos. However, this is a complex and often confusing area. And there are many systems of numerology.

As we have seen some numbers have particular significance in the Ageless Wisdom, notably the three representing the trinity and the three emanations of the logos and the seven, which underpins all esoteric systems. And numbers are also closely related to symbols.

## SPIRITUAL SELF-DEVELOPMENT

The fact that increasing numbers of people these days say they are more interested in being spiritual than in being religious represents a major change. The very many different groups and collectives within the New Age movement show a panoramic interest in numerous aspects of self-development from yoga and ta'i chi to meditation and mindfulness. These can be useful, although very many people in the West especially find meditation extremely difficult and struggle to tame what is often called 'the monkey mind' even for a moment.

Theosophy promotes meditation, service, brotherhood and renunciation as being key factors in developing the spiritual aspects of ourselves. In this competitive and separative world, the noble aspiration of brotherhood remains elusive.

Renunciation is an especially difficult notion for many people. Many spiritual traditions (including Theosophy) promote vegetarianism and abstinence from meat, alcohol, drugs and tobacco, although not all members observe these restrictions. There are also very often restrictions either total or partial on sexual activity. But ultimately these are only the outward, talked about aspects. Real renunciation is all about moving beyond the illusion that the physical plane and all its material temptations are all there is.

Madame Blavatsky highlighted altruism as perhaps the most important spiritual characteristic of all. In a greedy grasping world where selfishness abounds, putting others before self can seem quaintly old-fashioned. Nevertheless, it is crucial.

And even in this age where the lower self and the individual rule supreme, many people do continue to act in others' interests before their own. Many are unable to do so because the prevailing culture and belief-system in the West promotes notions of personal fulfilment through wealth, fame and other forms of glamour. Often in extreme circumstances such as war or natural disasters, more people work for the collective good rather than themselves. Unfortunately this situation does not always persist once the emergency is over.

So what does it mean to be spiritual? Does it mean living on a diet of beans in a remote cave for years on end with only a mantra and a loincloth for company? For 99 per cent of people spending a decade or two cross-legged high in the Himalayas is not only impractical but highly inappropriate. For all but a very few it would be a death sentence. We have to gear our spiritual quest to our circumstances including location, jobs and family commitments.

But there is much we can do. Contemplation, self-awareness and self-reflection are all useful means of gaining a closer insight into our inner worlds. Because let us not forget that the answers lie within ourselves – not somewhere out there. Understanding that the development of the everlasting Higher Self is more important than dwelling on the demands of the lower ego-based self is a major step forward for many people.

Since evolution is always such a bitter struggle through all kingdoms of nature and since we are involved in this long-term process, it is useful to cultivate key qualities such as resilience and persistence. Rather than being crushed by our inevitable failures, we should accept these as learning experiences. We should never be deterred but always determined to try again. Sometimes it is likened to being a spiritual warrior.

And this is vital because treading the spiritual path is no soft option. In every single case when an individual decides to somehow accelerate their spiritual awareness, life inevitably gets tougher and more challenging. We are faced with new problems and hurdles to overcome. As we expand our consciousness we find that we raise both positive and negative material to the surface. And indeed some of this is very negative indeed – the result of many lifetimes of less than altruistic activity.

Being on this path means putting yourself forward to be tested and finding the inner strengths to overcome and move forward.

*Above: Wanderer From The Resplendent City* (1933), by Russian painter, writer, archaeologist and Theosophist, Nicholas Roerich (1874-1947). Influenced by his wife Helena he became interested in Eastern religions and had a major impact on Theosophy and other modern esoteric traditions. In 1925 the couple embarked on an epic five year expedition across Asia, travelling to the Himalayas, remote parts of the Gobi desert and Tibet, where they were detained by the authorities for five months. Together they developed their own school of occultism known as Agni Yoga, which they described as a "system of living ethics". One of the finest artists of his generation, Roerich was also nominated for the Nobel Peace Prize on three occasions.

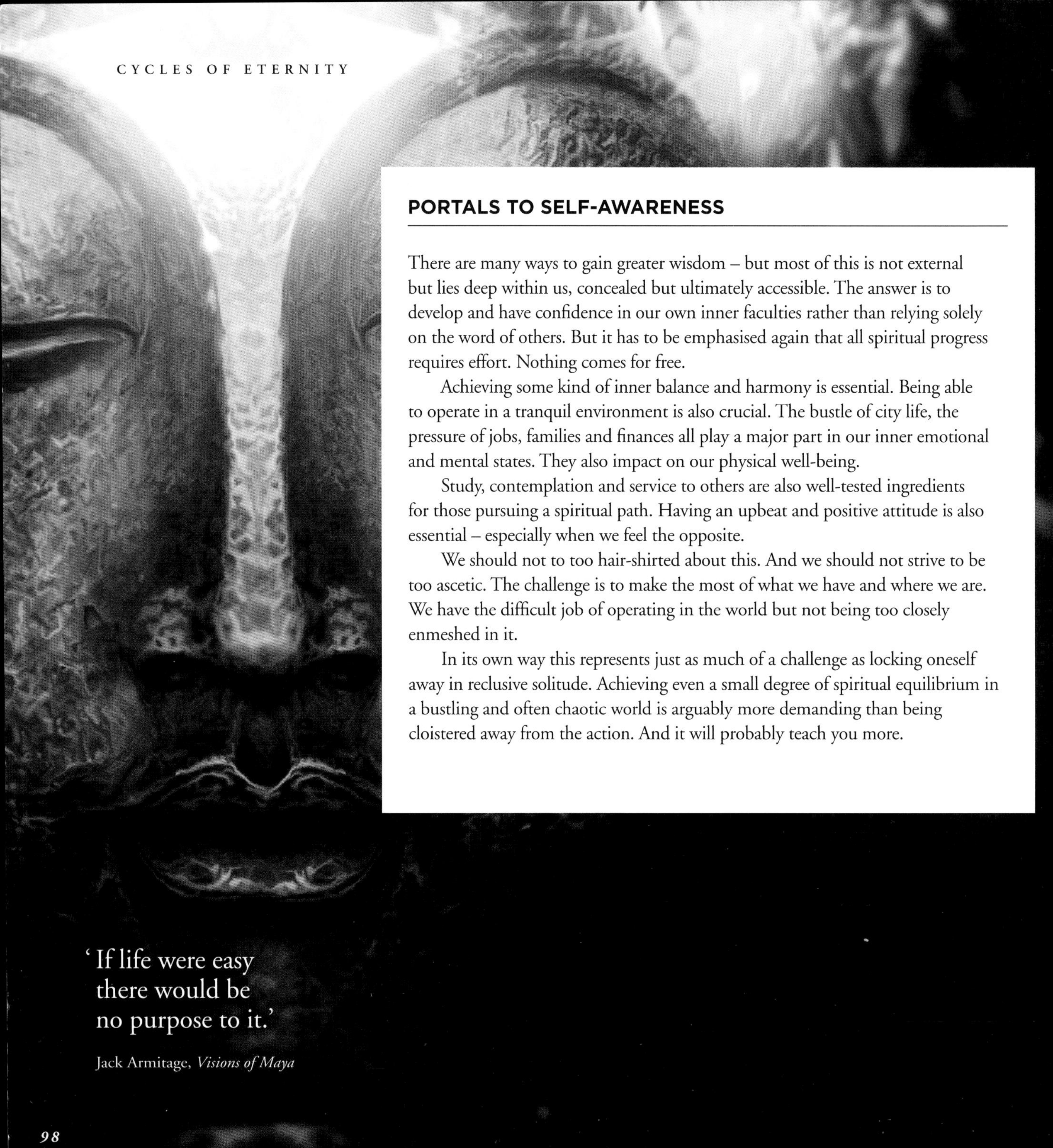

## PORTALS TO SELF-AWARENESS

There are many ways to gain greater wisdom – but most of this is not external but lies deep within us, concealed but ultimately accessible. The answer is to develop and have confidence in our own inner faculties rather than relying solely on the word of others. But it has to be emphasised again that all spiritual progress requires effort. Nothing comes for free.

Achieving some kind of inner balance and harmony is essential. Being able to operate in a tranquil environment is also crucial. The bustle of city life, the pressure of jobs, families and finances all play a major part in our inner emotional and mental states. They also impact on our physical well-being.

Study, contemplation and service to others are also well-tested ingredients for those pursuing a spiritual path. Having an upbeat and positive attitude is also essential – especially when we feel the opposite.

We should not to too hair-shirted about this. And we should not strive to be too ascetic. The challenge is to make the most of what we have and where we are. We have the difficult job of operating in the world but not being too closely enmeshed in it.

In its own way this represents just as much of a challenge as locking oneself away in reclusive solitude. Achieving even a small degree of spiritual equilibrium in a bustling and often chaotic world is arguably more demanding than being cloistered away from the action. And it will probably teach you more.

' If life were easy
there would be
no purpose to it.'

Jack Armitage, *Visions of Maya*

## OCCULTISTS: THE KEY PLAYERS

A few hard-line Theosophists, the so-called Back-To-Blavatskyites, insist that further revelations of the Ageless Wisdom ended with Helena P Blavatsky's death on 8th May 1891. This is extremely ironic given the fact that HPB herself would have railed violently against this idea. HPB's co-workers, Colonel Henry S. Olcott and William Q. Judge, were both accomplished esoteric authors and their works remain readable today.

The second generation of Theosophists, notably Annie Besant and Charles W. Leadbeater were even more prolific and tried to widen the accessibility of Ageless Wisdom ideas to a wider public. Some of their assertions remain controversial.

Other prominent 20th Century esotericists were also involved with the Theosophical Society for a time but went on to form their own movements. Rudolf Steiner, for example, formed his own variant called the Anthroposophical Society which is still active. Alice A. Bailey penned a series of two dozen books, mainly influenced by The Tibetan Master, Djwal Kuhl (more commonly known by the initials DK) and also set up the Lucis Trust. Her books, although challenging, remain highly influential. Krishnamurti, discovered as a young boy by Besant and Leadbeater and groomed to be the new world teacher, ultimately relinquished that role but went on to become a key spiritual voice.

### Revelations to come

HPB famously said that she had lifted only a tiny corner of the veil and revealed only a small proportion of the wisdom that could be released at that time. Since her death other details have emerged but much of our understanding remains fragmentary – and for good reason. Only a few have managed to absorb and understand the existing wisdom so it may be premature to unmask further secrets until we have a further grasp of these often difficult ideas – especially when human motives are often so venal and vicious.

Many occult writers have pointed out that frequently information is issued during the last quarter of every century. This was certainly true in HPB's time. The period 1875 to 1900 was a fertile time for new ideas – as was the period 1775 to 1800 and 1975 to 2000.

*Above, from left to right:* Annie Besant; C W Leadbeater; Rudolf Steiner; Alice Bailey; Jiddu Krishnamurti

'Magic opens the gates between the conscious and unconscious minds. The primary purpose of magic is connection.'

*Starhawk*

## LATENT HUMAN POWERS

Our conditioning often severely limits our belief in our own abilities and potential. This can restrict our capacities for exploration and personal expansion. And as we have seen, so can relying solely on our five physical senses.

But we have powers and areas of consciousness hidden deep within us that are largely unrecognised – and untapped. Those involved in studying the Ageless Wisdom have always been keen to learn more about these forces and potentialities in the hope of being able to use them practically – and beneficially.

For more than a century there has been intense interest in psychic powers such as telepathy (mind reading), clairvoyance and clairaudience (clear sight and hearing), psychokinesis (moving objects by mind power) and precognition (perceiving future events). Despite extensive research to prove the existence of psi phenomena, the 'noetic' sciences have been consistently mocked by academia. Even though many of these results have highlighted individuals with these powers, it seems that psi researchers face a much tougher statistical burden of proof than more accepted disciplines.

Alongside the existing physical senses, we are developing the new capacity of intuition (coinciding with our sixth higher vehicle of wisdom-intuition or buddhi). Some people possess this faculty already. Many people develop it as they get older. But in the next sixth sub-race – and throughout the Sixth Root Race far into the future – this will become standard issue.

What do we mean by intuition? Put

### Magic

Until recent centuries most people believed in some form of magic and hidden realms of beings. Indeed, despite the supposed rationalism of the age, many people still believe in 'supernatural' powers and the ability of some people to occultly control nature and her forces. The word supernatural is a misnomer. It simply refers to a realm we do not understand and cannot explain.

We all commit acts of magic every time we think. This happens both consciously and unconsciously. We are trying to get the hidden forces of the universe to bend to our will.

However, it is vital to make the distinction between two distinct types of magic. White magic is beneficial when used to help others and further the evolutionary plan. When used for any selfish or materialistic purpose whatsoever, this is black magic or the work of what is known as the Left Hand Path. So as we can see there is a lot of black magic around – and we should separate ourselves from it.

simply it is a form of perception which bypasses the mind itself, emanating from higher levels of being. This is knowledge beyond words and concrete concepts. Accompanying this faculty will be a greater degree of empathy and compassion.

Ancient Hindu writings speak of occult human powers which emerge with spiritual development known as *siddhis*, which means to attain perfection. These powers involve some awesome abilities including the disintegration of matter and the transportation of objects from one place to another. It is obvious that these powers should not be available to those lacking the purest of motives.

The eight siddhis are usually divided into two groups – those involving lower psychic and mental energies and those concerned with higher elements. They are:

1. Becoming as small as an atom
2. Assuming excessive lightness
3. Obtaining anything at will
4. Having an irresistible will
5. Increasing one's size
6. Achieving supremacy
7. Subduing one's own will
8. Suppressing desire

There is also what is known as etheric sight or vision. The etheric levels of matter are mainly invisible to the majority of people but there are individuals who claim to be able to penetrate this veil. Some highly-attuned esoteric writers and artists have described and depicted those entities who inhabit these etheric regions such as the lower elemental kingdoms (fairies, gnomes, tree-spirits etc) and the higher angelic or devic entities.

Many other people have a rudimentary ability to see these etheric energies – particularly on clear sunny days. Standing with your back to the sun and looking into a blue sky, etheric energies sometimes appear as faint swirling dark smudges.

We shall also develop other abilities of which we are as yet totally unaware. The result will be that over time human beings will be more empathic, co-operative and compassionate and less competitive, selfish and materialistic.

'Occult work for the welfare of all without thought of return or reward is white magic. It brings untold blessings to the world as well as to those by whom it is intelligently performed. Occult activity for material self-benefit, with the deliberately chosen motive of personal advantage, is black magic.'

Geoffrey Hodson, *Mind Radio*

***Above:*** Unseen by physical sight and existing on the etheric levels are hosts of entities such as nature spirits, devas and elementals.

## UNIVERSAL MYTHS

There are stories and legends from almost every culture in every age which bear striking resemblances to each other. They are usually told symbolically. It is as if they are part of a universal legend or myth.

Much religious material is allegorical. Jesus spoke in parables for the masses. *The Bhagavadgita* related by Krishna to Arjuna is the story of the human struggle set amongst an epic battle. The Greek myths especially tell many of the same stories but in a different way. And there are striking similarities in the background and circumstances of a number of key religious figures. Jesus and Krishna were both born on 25th December to virgin mothers called Mary (or its equivalent) and were crucified. Like the Greek God Dionysus they were placed in a manger after birth.

Some argue that there are close parallels between the life of Jesus and previous figures also including Baal, Bacchus, Hermes, Horus, Mithras, Orpheus, Osiris and Zoroaster. Common features of their lives include: having stars appear at their birth, being visited by Eastern magi, healing the sick, performing miracles (including turning water into wine), casting out demons, being betrayed, killed and resurrected.

## The forces of light and darkness

For countless aeons a battle has raged both on the inner planes and in the outer world between the forces of light and darkness – or more traditionally, between the forces of good and evil. By 'light' and 'good' we mean those forces which promote the grand evolutionary plan and those 'dark' or 'evil' energies which impede it and promote values of separateness, greed and personal power.

This epic and eternal struggle can be seen when we look back to the Atlantean period. During this Fourth Root Race there was a

schism between the Brothers of the Right Hand Path (sometimes known as Brothers of The Shining Face), who promoted white magic and those of the Left Hand Path known as Lords of the Dark Face who developed

sophisticated forms of black magic. These forces contributed to the progressive destruction of that great civilization.

This battle has continued ever since both openly and covertly. Sadly, it would often appear that the dark forces are in the ascendancy, spreading conflict, war, religious and political division, wealth inequalities and much more. However, it is hoped and believed that the powers of progress and evolution will ultimately prevail. We can all play a part in ensuring they do.

## THE REAL CAUSE OF DISEASE

Despite its huge advancement during the 20th Century medical science is still largely unaware of the root causes of disease because it focuses almost exclusively on the physical symptoms rather than deeper causes. Of course, psychological factors are increasingly accepted and there is a greater acceptance of 'psycho-somatic' causes produced by mental or emotional imbalances.

Disease *never* begins on the physical level, although this is where we become aware of it. It begins in our more subtle astral or mental bodies and is transmitted to the physical via its etheric double.

The causes of disease are numerous and complex. Although not widely accepted, illness and disease are often a result of our individual or collective karma and this may originate deep in history. Some of the widespread diseases we see today are very possibly the direct results of our ancestors.

For example, cancer, dementia and viruses could be the result of our Atlantean forebears malevolently meddling with nature.

Until we understand the basic principle that disease is not caused physically we shall neither understand it nor find effective cures – or better still preventative measures.

We are to some extent in uncharted waters never experienced before. Over the past century human beings have surrounded themselves with increasing doses not only of man-made radiation but huge amounts of electromagnetic energy – in our homes, in communications devices and in global infrastructures. How these may affect us over time remains unknown.

Homeopathy, herbalism, energetic medicine and other alternative and holistic therapies are still often ridiculed by mainstream medical science. And yet these may well hold some of the keys to a future less reliant on drugs, surgery and radiotherapy. And more fundamentally we need to understand that all disease and illness ultimately has a spiritual cause at the heart of it.

## YOGA

Although popular in the West, the ancient Hindu practice of yoga is still almost exclusively focused on body-posture (**hatha yoga**). In Sanskrit yoga means 'union' or 'conjunction' – its aim is to achieve at-one-ness with the divine spirit within. This involves achieving various higher states of consciousness and perception. The highest of these is known as **samadhi**. But it has much more than just a physical dimension, involving concentration, meditation and other mental techniques.

In the Indian tradition there are six different schools of philosophy each with its own branch of yoga. These ultimately lead to what is called **raja** or kingly yoga.

They are as follows:

1. Hatha yoga - control of the physical body through posture and breathing
2. Laya yoga - awakening of cosmic energies within the individual
3. Mantra yoga - steadying the mind
4. Jnana yoga - control of thought
5. Bhakti yoga - control of emotions by devotion to an ideal
6. Karma yoga - control of actions to achieve selflessness

It is recommended that hatha yoga especially is practised under the supervision of experienced practitioners. Individual experimentation with one's own psycho-spiritual energies can prove dangerous.

## DIVINATION

Throughout the ages there have been many forms of divination, fortune-telling and prediction. These range from casting rune stones, examining cloud patterns and scrying through crystal balls to numerology, dream analysis and reading tea leaves. Alongside astrology several ancient traditions now have a firm foothold in Western esoteric thought.

The Chinese *I Ching*, based on Taoist and Confucian ideas, is widely used as a system of prediction. It involves using coins or stalks to produce one of 64 six-line configurations known as hexagrams.

Tarot cards, whose origins go back to the Middle Ages and maybe much further back in time than that, are also popular. Normally consisting of 78 cards featuring a pictogram, a pack consist of 22 major trumps and 56 lesser cards in four suits.

Some people doubt the merit of these forms of 'prediction'. Others regard them as useful tools to access those realms beyond the immediate present and the purely physical.

## Beware gurus

Ever since the late 1960s when *The Beatles* famously met Maharishi Mahesh Yogi there has been a progressive guru-fication of The West. Often robed and bearded, these self-proclaimed purveyors of wisdom offer enlightenment – usually at a price. It is not unusual for some of the less scrupulous practitioners to drive round in Rolls Royces.

Those with strictly Eastern credentials have been especially well received and in some cases revered. Some have been shown to have had less than savoury – or spiritual – aspects to their characters.

Neither wisdom nor enlightenment should have a price tag. Those demanding money are always fakes.

Similarly, the New Age in the West has also spawned armies of supposed psychics, healers, channellers, counsellors, life-coaches, yoga experts and past-life regressionists – many with very dubious credentials. The true investigator of truth should be constantly wary – especially of grandiose claims.

As a general rule: question everything. No one has a monopoly on truth.

## SPEAKING PRACTICALLY

How can we incorporate this knowledge into our everyday lives?

While some of the Ageless Wisdom ideas are highly theoretical, often very technical and encompassing vast expanses of time, we can still use much of this ancient knowledge to aid our own evolution, widen our knowledge and gain a deeper intuitive understanding of who we are and where we are going. These ideas provide us with a long term perspective and an understanding that we are all on an endless voyage whether we understand it or accept it. We do not know the final destination of that immense journey – and in all likelihood it does not exist.

If we choose, we may decide not to be blinkered and hindered by the relatively mundane concerns of our current lives. We may decide to exercise our deeper powers of intuition and imagination and look beyond our present circumstances into those unseen worlds which interface with ours.

And having a wider grasp of the laws which run the universe naturally enhances our ability to actively participate, not only in our own personal evolution, but also that of the Earth and the solar system.

## KEY INDIVIDUALS

Throughout the course of history there are key individuals who appear and have a disproportionate effect on mankind. Avatars such as Buddha, Jesus and Krishna usher in important new messages for mankind. Pythagoras, Plato and Socrates re-shaped thought. Leonardo da Vinci, Francis Bacon and Einstein caused seismic disruptions to the way we see the world. Alexander the Great, Genghis Khan and other key military leaders re-drew the maps.

Alongside these towering names are the unseen ones who also influence history, world events and human thinking. Ever since we became human there have always been individuals more advanced than those they lived amongst. They bear radical, revolutionary and often very unwelcome ideas. They introduce concepts and notions so far ahead of popular consciousness that it may be decades or centuries before their ideas come to fruition.

FAMOSO·DOCTOR    PARESELSVS

These individuals are frequently seen as dangerous and a threat to the established order. This is why they are often marginalised or mocked as mad, reviled as agitators or persecuted as heretics. In many cases they are killed by the prevailing religion, state authorities or the mob.

They are the seed-planters whose ideas take time to gestate and grow and whose crops may not sprout for many generations. In the future it may be wise to take these people rather more seriously.

The Buddha *(above)* and the celebrated alchemist, scientific investigator and healer Paracelsus (1493-1541) *(left)* both shared the distinction of being outsiders with ideas generations ahead of their time. After relinquishing the luxurious trappings of princely life, Buddha ultimately found enlightenment but only after renouncing extreme personal austerity and finding a middle way. Paracelsus, an accomplished alchemist, healer and medical pioneer acquired many enemies with his radical theories and abrasive temperament. He is credited as being the father of homeopathy, the founder of toxicology and the man who first named the metal zinc. His medical philosophy was: 'The art of healing comes from nature, not from the physician. Therefore the physician must start from nature, with an open mind.'

## CONCLUSION

The key message of this book is that we are one life. We live in one world. We are intimately interconnected with and interdependent on all the kingdoms of nature and all planes of existence. We are participants in one evolution.

War, poverty, inequality – and above all ignorance – are the chief enemies – the weapons of bleak and insidious forces which still influence and interpenetrate the planet. The work to overcome these malign influences has continued for millennia and will no doubt continue for many more. Progress has been slow.

And yet our very survival depends on an unprecedented respect for and co-operation with all departments of nature – but principally among human beings themselves.

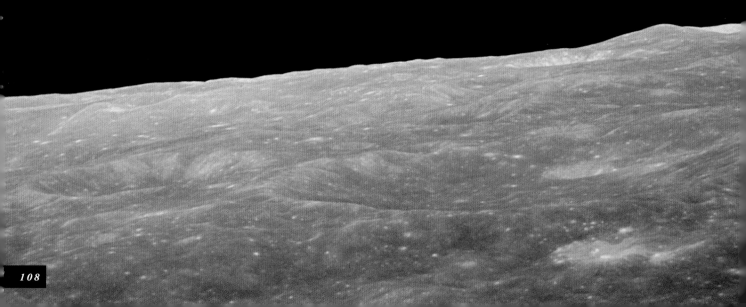

# AFTERWORD

We are always at some turning-point in evolution or human affairs. However, the 21st Century coincides with the major convulsions resulting from the transition from the Age of Pisces to the Age of Aquarius. This new cycle will set the tone for the next two thousand years and will be quite unlike anything humanity has experienced before. We find ourselves at a pivotal point in the re-shaping of the world because this major new realignment is based on a significant change and expansion in human consciousness. None of this is comfortable. And it manifests as crisis.

We can see this everywhere and at all levels – materially, mentally and spiritually. Outwardly the world is at war with itself. Much of this is religious and the warfare itself is becoming increasingly asymmetric. Divisions and conflicts, be they ideological, political, economic, social or religious, appear to be ripping humanity apart. This is because the previous patterns are crumbling. Change and periods of accelerated development are always accompanied by crisis and disorder.

Inwardly – and invisibly – human consciousness and behaviour is undergoing a radical transmutation within the flames of this upheaval and discord.

Nevertheless many people find themselves terrified, alienated or numbed by a world crackling with hatred, paranoia and violence. If we merely take a short-term view, it is all too easy to succumb to fear, negativity and a pervasive hopelessness. But if we take the more panoramic stand-point offered by the Ageless Wisdom we are able to see the present difficulties as merely a challenging phase in a greater cycle. Like everything else, this phase is only temporary. Eventually it will be superseded.

Transitions are never smooth and nor is life itself. The place where we find ourselves, Earth School, is a particularly gruelling and demanding environment. It has to be and this is why it is sometimes described as a learning planet. Of course, many cycles are beyond our control but an important part of our education during incarnation is learning about their effects so that we can become creative collaborators rather than passive bystanders.

The world may appear to be characterised by greed, violence and selfishness but it remains a beautiful place. And it is the *only* place for us to unfold our potential on the physical plane at this stage of human progress.

' Give a man a gun and he'll rob a bank. Give a man a bank and he'll rob the world.'

Anonymous

***Above:*** *Sunset on the River* (1805) by English landscape painter JMW Turner (1775-1851).

## FURTHER READING

Those interested in further exploration of the esoteric and occult ideas in The Ageless Wisdom may find the works of the authors listed below helpful. This is a very subjective selection of those individuals who have most inspired me and it is by no means a comprehensive list.

- Alice Bailey
- Douglas Baker
- Geoffrey A Barborka
- Annie Besant
- Edi Bilimoria
- Helena P Blavatsky
- Paul Brunton
- Gottfried de Purucker

- Geoffrey Farthing
- E L Gardner
- John Gordon
- Manly P Hall
- Max Heindel
- Geoffrey Hodson
- C Jinarajadasa
- William Q Judge

- Charles W Leadbeater
- Lynn McTaggart
- Henry S Olcott
- Joy Piper
- Arthur E Powell
- Rupert Sheldrake
- Rudolf Steiner

### The Theosophical Society - history and purpose

The Theosophical Society has had a huge impact on world thought, and continues its struggle towards universal brotherhood. The society was formed in New York in 1875 by Madame Blavatsky along with others including Colonel Henry S. Olcott and William Q. Judge. Its aim was to disseminate the occult knowledge gathered by HPB to a far wider public as well as introducing key aspects of Eastern esoteric spirituality to the West. Its early years were not successful and various rifts emerged – a trend which has continued regularly throughout the society's history. Various different strands of Theosophy exist today although broadly their teachings concur.

In the early 1880s the society moved its headquarters to Adyar near Chennai (formerly Madras) in India where it remains and has huge support in that country of so many spiritual traditions.

Currently, the society has around 25,000 members worldwide in 70 countries, although its influence is much wider, having been the catalyst for much of today's New Age movement.

The Society has three main aims:

1. To form a nucleus of the universal brotherhood of humanity, without distinction of race, creed, sex, caste or colour.
2. To encourage the study of comparative religion, philosophy and science.
3. To investigate unexplained laws of nature and the powers latent in man.*

* Originally, the third aim specified the 'psychic and spiritual' powers latent in man but this has since been amended.